TERENCE CONRAN

KITCHENS

THE HUB OF THE HOME

Clarkson Potter/Publishers
New York

DEDICATION This book is for Vicki, who has made the kitchen the happy hub of our home and cooks many wonderful meals for our friends, family, chefs and even Conran Shop buyers and directors.

INTRODUCTION

What do you do in your kitchen? More to the point, what don't you do? These days, the kitchen's role extends far beyond its original, central function as the place where food is stored, prepared, and cooked. Increasingly it doubles as an eating area, home office, playroom, entertainment zone, chatroom, domestic nerve center, and much else besides. In many households today, the kitchen forms the backdrop for a large part of what constitutes everyday living.

If one were to plot a day in the life of the average kitchen at the beginning of the twenty-first century, one might well record a constant stream of activity: preparing for the day at work or school...paying bills, writing lists, and carrying out other routine administrative chores...children playing under a parent's watchful eye or tackling homework at the kitchen table...socializing with friends...washing, drying, and ironing clothes...watching TV and listening to music...making phone calls and taking messages...having a quiet drink and swapping news at the end of the day...and all this in addition to making meals (and in many cases, sitting down to eat them).

The idea of the kitchen as fully fledged living space is relatively new. When I was working on my first Kitchen Book twenty-five years ago, we included the New York kitchen of George Lang, the celebrated Hungarian restaurateur and owner of Cafe des Artistes. The all-embracing nature of his kitchen, with its sound systems, television, office area, and wine storage, was fairly unusual for its time; today, such inclusiveness is far more expected. In my own kitchen in the country, there's a small table set aside where children can indulge in some of their messier creative pursuits, there's a television, but there's also an open fire. In my apartment in London, the whole of the upper floor is an open-plan kitchen/dining/living space: whoever's doing the cooking can watch TV across the room if they want, or talk to people while they prepare a meal.

Filled with light and air, this open kitchen, dining, and living area reflects the informality of contemporary lifestyles in its free arrangement of space. The L-shaped layout of cooking and preparation areas maximizes floor space and offers a neat way of integrating fixtures and appliances.

What is it about the kitchen that makes it attract roles with an almost centrifugal force? One answer must have something to do with the kitchen's fundamental association with food. A lot of the time we may eat to live, rather than live to eat, but the enjoyment of food goes beyond satisfying the basic need to keep body and soul together. Good food, particularly good food eaten in company, promotes a deep sense of well-being; it's simply one of life's greatest pleasures.

Statistics may show that we spend less time cooking today than ever before: professional working people especially are spending less than a couple of hours a week cooking for pleasure. But given the central importance of food in our lives, both physically and emotionally, perhaps it is not surprising that we're choosing to spend more of our time in the nurturing environment of the kitchen, even if that time is spent doing things other than cooking.

In a similar way, when so much of contemporary life is mediated via television or computer screens, part of the kitchen's appeal is that it can offer a means of grounding yourself in reality, a touchstone of tastes, smells, and textures that serves as an antidote

PREVIOUS PAGES: The enjoyment of food – and shared mealtimes – is one of the great pleasures of life. **BELOW:** Vernacular styles of kitchen decoration, design and fixtures still hold tremendous appeal, due to nostalgic associations with kitchens from our childhood. **BELOW RIGHT:** A more recent kitchen role model is the professional or catering style kitchen, which relies heavily on stainless steel fixtures, appliances, and surfaces.

to "virtual" experience. If the idea of the kitchen as a "reality" zone seems far-fetched, one has only to scan a shelf of bestselling cookbooks to see how often "real" comes up in the title. Indeed, many of today's most successful cookbooks and most popular cooking programs have little to do with ingredients and recipes; they are celebrations of sensuality and appetite. Kitchens, in this sense, are not promoted as places where, of necessity, we have to be — they're places where we want to be.

Pressure on time may also help to account for the kitchen's new inclusiveness. When time is short, people are less inclined to stand on ceremony. The old notion of the kitchen as the "downstairs" domain of the cook and her kitchenmaids, only visited with some trepidation by the mistress of the house, disappeared along with the servant class well over half a century ago. For a while, when kitchens became the housewife's exclusive realm, the distinction between the "working" parts of the home and those areas where guests were welcomed and entertained remained in place. But as more and more women have gone out to work and the average household has shrunk to variations on the theme of the family unit, kitchens have necessarily emerged from behind the scenes. If the time you spending cooking means less time for relaxing, entertaining, and simply being with your family, the idea of retreating behind closed doors to prepare a meal can be very unappealing. Nor does anyone particularly want to rush home from work and shut themselves away to fret anxiously over ingredients and cooking times while everyone is having a good time somewhere else.

As the kitchen has absorbed roles, it has also inevitably redefined the way we use space. A kitchen that could comfortably accommodate at least some of the roles sketched out above is necessarily on the large side. But at the same time, space is increasingly at a premium these days and many people find themselves settling for homes that are smaller than they would like. The solution to this apparent dilemma has inevitably involved a little creative interior shape-shifting. As more of what comprises everyday living has migrated into the kitchen, the kitchen has encroached first on the dining room and secondly on living areas in general. "Kitchen-diners" have long been a common planning arrangement in many homes; today, however, the development of this concept has led to the single multipurpose space that embraces a range of activities, from relaxing and eating to cooking and working.

BELOW LEFT: Kitchens are the hardest-working areas in the home and consequently demand precision planning. Sound planning becomes even more critical when available space is tight. This kitchen, fitted along the length of a wall, doubles as a spatial divider.

BELOW RIGHT: The sleek, seamless fitting of this compact kitchen area, integrated into a narrow corridor immediately off a workspace, is the ultimate in reticence.

ABOVE: The kitchen as sleek workbench makes an almost sculptural statement in a loft space. Such modular designs liberate kitchen planning from walls and partitions and are increasingly popular. This "kitchen cube" incorporates oven, fridge, dishwasher, cooktop, and sink in a single, streamlined unit; the stainless steel top can be slid across to serve as a table or additional preparation space.

In this sense, one might almost say that the "kitchen" as a separate, isolated entity has disappeared, shrunk to a functional zone within a space where activities flow freely from one area to the next.

One impetus for this change has arisen with the vogue for "loft living," even when the "loft" is little more than an average-size apartment. Open-plan kitchen/living/dining areas, also known as "great rooms," have been popular here for a considerable time, particularly on the West Coast, but the popularity of open-plan lofts in cities has brought the combined kitchen/dining room/living room into the homes of a much broader spectrum of the population.

In the more literal sense, kitchens in some cities are disappearing altogether. Many New York apartments designed for professionals omit any kitchen facilities at all, on the assumption that childless affluent singles prefer to eat out all the time, a trend aided and abetted by the fact that restaurant-going plays a central role in many people's social lives. I can sympathize with those who wish to simplify their lives to such an extent and I can appreciate that in dense metropolitan areas like New York it makes sense to maximize space, but I personally would find it very difficult to distinguish between an apartment without a kitchen and a hotel room. Much as I enjoy hotels, I wouldn't want to live in one.

For me and, I suspect, many people, kitchens indeed are the hub of the home. I would also argue that they are the heart of family life. A kitchen that is big enough to live in and eat in prevents families from fragmenting into a collection of individuals who eat their pre-prepared meals alone in front of the television. (With many households owning more than one set, it may not even be the same television.) The kitchen is one of the few remaining places where families can be guaranteed to spend at least some time together; where children can learn how to eat, what to eat, and (hopefully) how to behave; where a little of the ceremony and ritual of shared mealtimes can be enacted.

Only a few decades ago, the "dream" kitchens of popular imagination were chiefly defined in terms of their "style" or the sophistication with which they were equipped. In the 1950s and early 1960s, the kitchens that everyone wanted were dazzling models of efficiency, with their wipe-clean surfaces, built-in cabinets, and new domestic appliances. By the 1970s country kitchens were the height of fashion, featuring warm, woody surfaces – we sold plenty of them at Habitat — mutating into the more self-consciously nostalgic or period looks of the 1980s. Then, inspired by the restaurant boom and the rise in eating out as a social activity, wannabe professional-style kitchens, all in gleaming stainless steel, became status symbols of the last decade.

Today, however, I suspect that dream kitchens are visualized very differently. On the basis of some very unscientific research, it appears that what people want is a kitchen that suits the way they want to live. "Big and bright," "somewhere large enough to live in and entertain in," "a big table to eat on and work on," "a door open to the backyard," "everything at hand," "not too neat — Post-it notes (stickies) or magnets on the fridge" were some of the answers from this informal survey. The picture that emerges is not a kitchen taken straight from a manufacturer's brochure, but a simple, calm, and welcoming place at the heart of the home.

This new emphasis on kitchen living does not mean you can neglect the kitchen's prime function. For kitchens to be enjoyable and pleasant places, they must, first of all, work well, which means integrating servicing with the layout of appliances, providing enough storage space and areas for preparation, getting the lighting right, and a host of other practical considerations. Once these basic elements have been properly considered, everything else is more likely to fall into place.

In many ways, life is over-complicated these days. The kitchen should be one place where we remember to keep it simple.

ABOVE LEFT: This kitchen suspended from the underside of a mezzanine represents a somewhat unusual way of maximizing floor space and providing uninterrupted views, a service core literally at the heart of the home. Sliding panels screen working areas when not in use. **ABOVE RIGHT:** Borrowing heavily from the science lab, these plug-in gas rings on their tiled base provide a cooking set-up that offers optimum flexibility. The design is a prototype.

Planning
and Design

The kitchen is the most intensively used space in the home and the one place where we are spending more and more time. Thoughtful planning and careful design are therefore essential before you undertake any alteration or purchase any new equipment.

A well-designed kitchen will allow you to move smoothly from task to task in a logical sequence and to work comfortably, safely, and efficiently. It will also allow you to integrate a wide variety of appliances and equipment seamlessly into your living space. The key is to create a blueprint that incorporates every requirement for you and your circumstances, while allowing flexibility for future change.

BELOW: Everyday cooking utensils and basic ingredients can be as effective as a display of artfully arranged objects, and this way the most regularly used items are also within easy reach of the cook. **RIGHT:** Architectural features are a good starting point for kitchen design. This kitchen retains a strong sense of character and individuality that is enhanced by the laboratory-style workbench. **FAR RIGHT:** A split-level island unit makes sound ergonomic sense. The lower section is used for cooking and preparing food while guests can perch on bar stools at the higher level.

The basics of good planning are the same whether you want to change your kitchen dramatically – a rip-it-out-and-start-again project with new cabinets, appliances, flooring, counters and so on – or if you just feel like an update or cosmetic improvements. Both require financial commitment and planning if you are to achieve the optimum design. To reach the definitive layout, you need to review all the options, taking into account space, function, and budget.

If you decide to seek professional advice from an architect or a kitchen designer, you will still need to have a firm idea of what you want from your kitchen and what decorative style you prefer. Good research and thorough preparation are therefore indispensable. That's not to say you shouldn't follow your creative instincts, but hasty decisions can often lead to expensive mistakes.

A good design will create a good-looking kitchen tailormade to your way of working. It will also save money by helping you to allocate your budget effectively. Consider all the options and the benefits will be long-lasting – a stylish and practical kitchen that you will enjoy for years to come.

ADDING VALUE

A good kitchen is often at the top of a potential homebuyer's wish list, after location and price. In fact, installing a new kitchen is almost guaranteed to add value to the property, more so than any other home improvement, and will also help to sell the house more quickly. However, it is important to reconcile the cost of improvements with the resale value it adds. If you plan to move on in a few years, think carefully about expenditure; although a kitchen does add value to your home, it is rarely equivalent to the kitchen cost. The amount you spend must also relate to the value of the property and you are unlikely to recoup your money if you put a top-of-the-range kitchen into a small, relatively inexpensive house.

The most important consideration is that you choose a kitchen you will enjoy using. However, it is wise to make changes that reflect mainstream taste now that a kitchen has become such a selling point – your successors may not be as enamored with a bubblegum-pink kitchen as you are, though paint colors are easy to change. Choose neutral shades and classic-style cabinets rather than quirky fittings and state-of-the-art appliances. Plan the kitchen so that it is not so idiosyncratic that someone else can't use it. That said, making a kitchen nondescript is also inadvisable, so if you live in an older home, try to retain the character and period details such as original glass-front cupboards, moldings and wooden countertops, which often end up as financial as well as aesthetic assets.

You may want to update your current kitchen rather than shoulder the cost of a full refit. A solid, well-organized kitchen inherited from a previous owner can be improved by simple, cosmetic changes such as painting cabinet doors or filling open shelving with your own collection of china.

LEFT: A huge, weathered table is the focus of family activity and the inspiration for this rustic kitchen. The kitchen cabinets screen off the utility area and are coated with latex chalkboard paint, while the black rubber flooring injects a hint of metropolitan style into the otherwise simple scheme.

Replacing tiles, countertops, and new cabinet door handles can transform a tired-looking kitchen for little outlay and are effective ways of personalizing the room. You could also improve your kitchen layout and storage capacity by moving a radiator, the sink, or existing appliances.

PLANNING FROM SCRATCH

The most crucial question to consider is whether the kitchen is in the right place. For instance, it may make sense to move the kitchen from the ground floor to the basement so that it leads on to the backyard, thus making it easier to transfer food for outdoor dining and barbecues and hang laundry on a clothesline. You can also keep an eye on young children playing outside while preparing meals. Alternatively, moving the kitchen to the top floor may offer better light and space, while bedrooms may benefit from being relocated to a cool basement. Design the layout of your house around how you live – if the kitchen is the center of your home, reshuffle the rooms accordingly, so the kitchen gets the best location and optimum natural light.

If you are fortunate enough to be able to choose which direction your kitchen will face, in a new house or a total refurbishment, it is a good idea to orientate it toward the sunrise. This will flood the room with morning light, and give you an opportunity to utilize the solar energy.

Even if you don't relocate the kitchen to another room, you may want to restructure the space by removing or moving walls, windows, or doors. If you are considering any structural alterations, always seek professional advice.

Whether your kitchen is a separate room or an open-plan, inclusive layout, it should blend smoothly with entrances, halls, and staircases. If the kitchen leads on to the backyard, you may consider adding a porch or mudroom to keep coats, umbrellas, and boots out and the heat in, or build on an extra pantry if the kitchen is north-facing. And if your kitchen is the main "corridor" from the entrance of the house to the backyard and doubles as a busy thoroughfare, it may be wise to add another back exit elsewhere. If this is impossible, make sure the primary work area is sited away from the two doors and out of the way of passing traffic. Professional advice will often cast a fresh perspective on space and location.

When it comes to good kitchen planning, bigger isn't necessarily better. Layout is more important than size, and large kitchens are only practical if the appliances and storage cabinets are ergonomically arranged. A smaller kitchen does not mean compromising on function or sacrificing style. And in practical terms, a smaller total surface area means that you will have to spend less on materials and so can afford better-quality ones.

Permissions

If you intend to add a room or alter any part of the front elevation, you may need a building permit. It is a good idea to contact the appropriate authorities at a very early stage,

even before commissioning any drawings or plans. They can indicate what is acceptable and what is not, and in most cases, advise whether a building permit is required, saving you time and possibly money.

If you intend to convert a unused basement into a kitchen, you may have to notify the planning authorities of a change of use. And if you live in an historic building, you will need a permit for any alteration that affects either its character or its setting. Any structural alterations – for example, putting a door in a structural wall or removing a chimney breast – may require approval, depending on your local building codes. If you hire an architect or interior designer, it is their responsibility to seek such permission. If you do the work yourself, start with the building inspector and ask to be referred to any other organization whose permission is required.

ABOVE: A chrome teakettle and toaster are the only signs of ornamentation in this open-plan kitchen, which is part of a loft apartment in a 1920s warehouse conversion. A simple bar separates the kitchen from the dining area. **RIGHT:** The well-planned kitchen insures that the cook has everything at hand. Here, a seemingly effortless mix of freestanding cabinets and appliances and open shelving belies the meticulous planning and organization that have gone into the design.

WORKING OUT PRIORITIES

Before you start planning you need to determine your priorities and anticipate future needs. By looking at your style of life, the architecture of your house, and your cooking habits, you will gradually build up an idea of the style and design of kitchen you want. Then ask yourself whether you would you feel happier handing the project, either partly or fully, over to a professional.

Function

▸ How regularly is your kitchen used?

▸ What activities will you do there: food preparation and cooking; food storage; everyday eating; entertaining; laundry; office and schoolwork; watching television?

▸ Who uses the kitchen? Are you a single person, a professional couple without children, or part of a large family?

▸ Do you want a designated eating area, whether it's a table, a breakfast bar, or an island unit?

▸ Are you a serious cook or do you feed yourself from cans, packages, and pre-prepared food?

▸ Do you keep pets who eat or sleep in the room?

▸ Can the kitchen be comfortably used, or adapted for use, by a less-able or elderly person?

Space

▸ Look at the size and shape of your kitchen. Is it big enough for the activities, appliances, and storage you require, without restricting movement? If not, is it feasible to enlarge the space or build an addition, taking into account your budget and timescale?

RIGHT: The kitchen is the multifunctional hub of the home, a place where meals can be eaten and children can play without interrupting the kitchen's primary function – cooking, a shift marked here by the change in flooring.

FAR RIGHT: Natural light is a key feature of the kitchen. This dark space has been opened up with a large skylight, which lets daylight flood in. White cabinet fronts, pale flooring, and a painted ceiling bounce the light into dark corners.

► How many doors are there? Do they open inward or outward? Are they correctly placed or could any be repositioned to better advantage?

► Can you design a new kitchen without undermining the original character of your home? Have you considered the architectural features in the room such as pillars or chimney breasts?

► Consider the aspect of the kitchen. How much natural light is there in the room? If there is little or none, consider ways of obtaining or increasing the amount of daylight with a roof skylight, sliding glass doors, or full-length windows.

► Is there access to an outside wall for ducting?

► Can it be naturally ventilated?

Needs

► List what you like and dislike about your existing kitchen, then list the qualities of your ideal kitchen. Evaluate what is an essential improvement and what you may be able to do without.

► What are your priorities: a view from your kitchen window; more light; plenty of countertop space and storage; a family-friendly room; direct access to outside areas?

► What are your favorite kitchen styles? Start a kitchen design file for your ideas and start collecting brochures, magazine cuttings, and samples of tiles, flooring, and paint colors that you like.

► Which kitchen appliances do you want? A built-in oven or freestanding range; refrigerator and freezer; dishwasher; microwave; garbage disposer? Could laundry appliances be moved elsewhere to free more space?

► Make a list of all your small appliances to help you decide how many electric outlets you will need and where they should go. Evaluate whether you actually use all of these appliances and how often. Infrequently used ones could be stored out of the kitchen if storage space is limited.

► How much storage space will you need for dried goods, pots and pans, small appliances; wine; cutlery and china? Do you want any or all items on display, everything tucked away in cupboards, or a combination of both?

Safety

Most accidents at home occur in the kitchen, so try to incorporate these planning precautions.

► Install ranges and cooktops away from windows – drafts may extinguish gas flames and curtains may catch alight. Gas stoves with a flame failure device will cut off the supply if the flame is accidentally extinguished.

► Choose a non-slip material for floors.

► Place heavy items such as casserole dishes and small appliances in the lower cabinets or on shelves. Lighter items like glassware can be put in upper cabinets while deep drawers with non-slip bases allow crockery to be stored without sliding as the drawer is opened and closed.

► If paint was applied to a surface in your kitchen before 1980, there is a 50 percent chance it contains lead. There are kits available from home centers if you want to check.

► Cords on small appliances should be shortened or replaced with curly ones to prevent from children pulling on any cord that might overhang the counter. Never trail cords across a sink or stove or install electrical switches and outlets near a water source.

► Flank cooking areas with a heat-resistant countertop.

► Choose rounded or axis corners on countertops.

► Insure work surfaces and cooking areas are well lit.

► Fit child locks on any drawers and doors containing chemicals or other potentially dangerous objects. Every kitchen should contain a fire extinguisher and fire blanket.

► If you do any deep-fat frying, learn how to put out a fat fire (smother the flames with a damp cloth).

ERGONOMICS

When it comes to planning your kitchen, ergonomics is a key consideration. The most important rule here is the "work triangle," a concept worked out by ergonomic studies in the early 1950s (and based on research conducted in the 1920s to improve industrial efficiency). These studies showed that the overall distance between your sink, fridge, and stove – the three chief activity centers in the kitchen – should not be too great. Since nearly all the manual labor done in the kitchen involves laps between the three, the objective is to make the distances between them comfortable. The study established carefully measured distances between these three primary kitchen areas to optimize convenience and safety. Ideally, an imaginary line joining the sink, fridge, and stove should measure no more than 20ft in total, although the sides of the triangle can vary according to the size and shape of the room. However, the distance between each work zone should be at least 3ft. If the distances are too far, you will waste time and energy moving from one end of the kitchen to the other. If the distances are too short, working in the kitchen becomes cramped and uncomfortable.

Divide your kitchen into sectors. Start with the food storage area, which should include the fridge and ideally cabinets and a work surface for preparation. Next is the cooking area, where the oven and cooktop should be flanked by counters suitable for placing hot pans on. The sink area should also include nearby storage for crockery and cutlery after washing the dishes.

The most important workspace in the kitchen lies between the sink and the stove, because that is where the most activity takes place. Situate the main food preparation area between the two – it should be the longest stretch of

ABOVE LEFT: Tambour shutters create an "appliance garage" for storing small electrical equipment, keeping long, trailing cords out of reach.

RIGHT: Custom-made, floor-to-ceiling cabinets are away from the work triangle, but with the multi-depth upper cabinets, maximize storage space.

LEFT: This kitchen incorporates a small curved peninsula to provide extra work surface and a mini-breakfast bar where friends or family can be entertained while you cook.

ABOVE: The sleek functionality of this galley kitchen has been fully optimized with careful planning, light colors, and plain, hardwearing materials like glass backsplashes.

continuous countertop in the kitchen and large and durable enough to serve a meal. Neither the sink nor the cooktop should be relegated to the corner of the room. Instead, place them at least 16in from the corner so you can work over them without banging elbows or pans on the wall.

Basic rules

Depending on the size and shape of the kitchen, dimensions of the triangle will vary, but here are the basic concepts.

▸ Since plumbing is the most expensive item to change, start with the current position of the sink and plot the layout from there. Group laundry equipment and a dishwasher together and near the sink for easy plumbing.

▸ Place a counter near the fridge for so you can move food in and out quickly, reducing the amount of time the fridge door remains open.

▸ The range or cooktop should be placed along an exterior wall, making it easy to install an efficient ventilation system. Or, if cooking appliances are fitted in a central island unit, install an overhead canopy hood.

▸ Avoid interrupting the flow of the work triangle with tall cabinets. It is better to group tall ones together at the end of a run of countertops in an area outside of the triangle.

▸ Allow plenty of space for appliance doors to open. Dishwashers, front-loading washing machines, and dryers need more room because you have to stand in front or to the side of the door to fill and empty the machine.

Standard dimensions

The height of a kitchen is as important as the layout. Cabinets, shelves, and drawers should be designed to minimize bending down and reaching up, especially for frequently used items and basic food supplies. Very wide, deep drawers below the work surface are ideal. These huge pull-outs – ranging from 3ft to 6ft wide – provide capacious storage and glide out smoothly with one pull.

It should not be assumed that the height of counters must be completely uniform throughout your kitchen. Ideal working heights vary not only for different people but for different activities. The standard elbow-height of 35in is recommended for general food preparation, but delicate, complex jobs such as frosting a cake, need a higher surface as you have to give it closer attention. For heavier tasks such as kneading bread or rolling out pastry, where you must put your full weight over the task, a lower level would be more convenient; say 30in. The cooktop can also be lowered so you can see into the pans during cooking, stir easily, and lift heavy pots off comfortably.

While it is a convenient advantage to have a countertop tailored to suit your height and the specific tasks you may carry out, counters that vary too much in height can cause jarring visual disharmonies and can also overly complicate small kitchens, especially where there isn't much countertop space. Equally, tailoring your kitchen too much to one specific individual may restrict other users, including any future owner. It may be simpler and cheaper to build up the counter with a thick slab of wood for chopping and use a tabletop with a marble slab for pastry making.

KITCHEN LAYOUTS

Don't be alarmed if your new kitchen is the size of a shoebox; efficient use of space depends more on how it is laid out than on how much there is. There are six basic layouts that, working within the work triangle, will create an efficient, practical kitchen.

The **SINGLE-LINE** kitchen is best utilized in narrow rooms and is suitable for one or two people to use at once. For this layout to work as an efficient kitchen, you ideally need 10ft of uninterrupted wall space. Use built-in or built-under appliances to exploit all available space and allocate as much countertop as possible – the longest stretch should be between the oven and sink. Sliding cabinet doors may be more practical than hinged ones, while extra storage can be provided by narrow glass shelves between the counter and upper cabinets. If it is part of an open-plan space, consider screening off the kitchen with sliding or folding doors, to contain cooking smells or hide dirty saucepans.

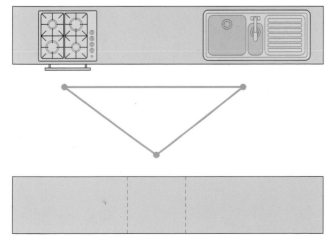

The **GALLEY** kitchen with two facing lines of cabinets provides the most efficient use of space, and is the layout most coveted by professional chefs. A galley is comprised of counters on both sides of the room with a corridor down the middle. There should be at least 4ft of space between facing cabinets to allow comfortable access to the lower ones; a fold-down table can be incorporated at one end. Try to add as much natural light as possible, especially if the kitchen is located in a dark or narrow corridor.

The **L-SHAPED** kitchen is a versatile layout with cabinets along two adjacent walls. It works well with a sitting area that is also integrated into the same room and also overcomes any shortage of wall space.

The cooktop, fridge, and sink should ideally be separated by a countertop to provide adequate preparation space. Dead space in the corner can be maximized with a carousel or Magic Corner cupboard.

The **U-SHAPED** kitchen utilizes three full walls of a room space. It is safe and efficient, offers maximum storage and workspace, and suits both large and small rooms. In a small kitchen, however, make sure there is at least 6ft in the middle. The only weak point of this plan is that separate work centers can become remote. To prevent this from happening in long, thin rooms or very large kitchens, the work triangle should be restricted to the bottom of the U.

The **ISLAND** kitchen is only suitable for large rooms with a lot of available floor space. An island can be introduced into a large U-shaped or L-shaped kitchen to give a more compact work triangle. Islands create a separate working area and can be used for storage, a cooktop, or a sink, but bear in mind that plumbing and electrical connections will need to run under the floor. Guests can chat to the cook working in the kitchen but will stay out of the way seated on the other side of the island. An island unit can also create a feeling of openness, although careful planning is needed to prevent wasted journeys around it. At its simplest, the island may just be a wooden table around which several people can gather to do the peeling, chopping, and slicing.

The **PENINSULA** kitchen is another way of creating a compact kitchen area in a large room (see page 28). The jutting-out counter can be used as a breakfast bar or to house one of the key activity areas.

BEYOND THE TRIANGLE

Don't feel you must adhere rigidly to the work triangle rule. It is a good basic principle of organization, but today's kitchens function very differently from those of 50 years ago. The human element is equally if not more important than scientific principles. Only you will be able to identify your cooking habits, your storage needs, and where you like to eat, and if these conflict with the work triangle, you can choose to ignore it. It is better to get the correct layout for your needs than to stick rigidly to a rule.

For example, if you consider cooking to be an inclusive activity, it may make sense to widen the work triangle and add a second sink and work area so that family and friends can join in. This is also a good way of encouraging children to get involved with cooking from an early age. However, if you want to prevent guests from helping with the cooking, the kitchen should be laid out so friends are given subtle spatial clues about where they can or cannot linger. The easiest way to do this is to incorporate an island with seating at one end, away from the work area. A parent may want to situate the cooktop so he or she can keep their eyes on the cooking and on the children in an adjoining room at the same time.

The fridge is the most flexible of the three activity centers in the work triangle. You may choose to move it out of the optimum triangle, since many cooks prefer to take all the ingredients out of cold storage at one time, before they start cooking.

RIGHT: Relaxed and comfortable, the full-length windows in this kitchen instill a sense of eating outdoors and provide a backdrop of natural color. Seating at the far end of the work surface encourages guests to linger as you cook, but keeps them out of your way.

case study:
THE U-SHAPED KITCHEN

Architect-designed kitchens sound expensive, but they can offer surprisingly good value for money, as well as the opportunity to reconfigure space. Here, the starting point for architect Steve Turvil was the creation of a flat-roofed addition linking the side of the house and the boundary wall and connecting the kitchen with the rest of the house. A postwar lean-to which had extended the original kitchen out into the yard was demolished, making a more usable rectangular outdoor space instead of the former L-shape.

LEFT: One of the client's stipulations for the new design was the retention of the Aga range. In the old layout, the Aga had been located in the corner. Here it is built in between cabinets. Instead of the window being blocked up, it was fitted with sandblasted glass to provide a natural light source. **RIGHT:** Looking across the new family room/dining area into the kitchen, which is set down a step. Flooring in the family room is solid oak, and in the kitchen is limestone inset with small slate squares. The large wooden chopping board slides off the slate counter to reveal additional gas burners.

LEFT: The worktop and draining board are made of oak, while cantilevered oak shelves wrap around a pier, making a visual connection between kitchen and family room. Some of the shelves are slatted for stacking plates. Because the client wanted to retain a large bullet trash bin, the shelves are set at a higher level than the counter to accommodate the bin tucked underneath. **ABOVE:** Custom-designed vegetable drawers in perforated aluminum with oak handles. **RIGHT:** The double-doored fridge is built into the wall. Additional storage space is provided by a generous walk-in pantry, built into what was formerly a corridor. Other cabinets are faced with spray-lacquered moisture-resistant medium-density fiberboard.

DESIGN SERVICE

Most kitchen specialists offer a free design and planning service. However, some companies, particularly the upscale, custom manufacturers, will view the plan as their own property until you have agreed to buy a kitchen from them. This means that you can use that kitchen design only if you choose that company.

The planning process usually begins with a house visit to measure the room, although most of the large home centers will ask you to do this yourself (see Resources, page 213 on how to measure accurately).

Then the retailer should discuss in detail what you want from the kitchen. This should include a whole series of questions to ascertain what you like and dislike about your current kitchen (if there is one), to find out about your lifestyle of life and priorities, and to set the budget for the work you want done (see Resources, page 211). Of course, as well as the functional element, there will also be a question of aesthetics. What style of kitchen do you prefer? What colors, materials, and decoration do you lean toward? What is the decor of the rest of your house? Have you seen or do you have any pictures of kitchens that you admire? It will help and save time if you have as many answers ready as soon as you meet with the kitchen designer, retailer, or architect. A specialist is there to suggest options, offer expert advice, and answer your queries or concerns, but at the end of the day it is your kitchen, and only you know what will suit you. Similarly, be wary of a specialist who doesn't ask you any or enough relevant questions. This is the groundwork on which your future kitchen will rest, and one instance where more is definitely more.

Once you and your designer have ascertained exactly what you want from your kitchen, and how it should look, the dimensions can be translated into a scale plan, either as a hand-drawn illustration or as a computerized assimilation. Most kitchen specialists now offer CAD (computer-aided design) planning packages which give you an accurate perspective of how your finished kitchen will look, as a color photo-realistic 3-D plan on a computer screen. As well as giving you a good idea of how the kitchen will function and look, changes can be made quickly and simply. For example, cabinet doors can be swapped for doors of a different style, or wall cabinets replaced with open shelving if the room appears too cramped. Virtual reality software is also available, and allows you to "walk around" your kitchen and view every perspective in simulated daylight and dusk.

When you are happy with the layout, you can take home a printout to consider, before making any final decisions.

Working with an architect

Architects don't just design vast corporate office blocks or expensive loft apartments, they also remodel houses – and parts of houses. Commissioning an architect to design your kitchen is a particularly good idea if you are planning to transform your whole house. This way the kitchen will form part of an overall blueprint that flows with the rest of the structure. An architect can also sort out any building permits and local building regulations, help find other professionals, and get the best price from builders.

Magazine features, architectural organizations, and personal recommendation are the best routes to find an architect. Call a few and look at portfolios and previous jobs. Don't be put off by the preconception that architects are expensive. An architect's fee depends on the service the client requires. A full service involves initial meetings to discuss what you want and how the architect perceives the project to work. Then, a brief is drawn up covering design, function, running costs, budget, and timing, accompanied by sketches and detailed plans. After obtaining a building permit, they will monitor the subcontractors to make sure the work and materials are up to standard. For this type of service an architect will usually charge a percentage of the final contract sum. The fee will also depend on whether the project is a new-build or an alteration to an existing building. You could save money by dealing with the building work yourself, but if something goes wrong, an architect will have the objectivity and expertise to deal with it.

A fully equipped island unit with a sink, cooktop, and plenty of counter space has been planned with precision, creating a one-piece kitchen that blends unobtrusively into this large, sunny room. Good design is essential in a big space to avoid wasted journeys around the island.

UNIVERSAL DESIGN

Few kitchens are single-person operations. The people who use your kitchen will all vary: tall and short, old and young, able and less able.

Universal design, also called multi-generational design, bridges the gap. It is a loose blueprint for a kitchen that can be used regardless of age or disability; whether it's deterring a four-year-old from scampering up a chair or enabling an 80-year-old with arthritis to turn on the faucet. The basic principle is to amplify ability rather than handicap the less able. With careful layout and sound advice, a universal kitchen will let older people remain in their family home and also allow grandchildren to experiment with cooking. At the same time, the kitchen can be a beautiful and ergonomic space for all generations to use.

ABOVE: A mid-height, side-opening oven suspended from the countertop and combined with movable cabinets mean that this kitchen is not only stylish, but also flexible and practical for a less mobile user.

RIGHT: A trio of movable cabinets hase been custom built to fit the space below the countertop. Each one can be pulled out to create extra counter space and make cleaning more accessible.

Today most skilled designers and architects should be able to create a good-looking, universal kitchen without its feeling institutionalized. Look at as many kitchens as you can, talk to friends and advisers, and, if possible, visit a disabled living center where there will be kitchens on display.

To allow for comfortable wheelchair turning, a space of not less than 55 x 55in is required where toe recesses are provided under the lower cabinets; 59 x 59in where they are not. It is equally important that there should not be too much space so that the user does not have to maneuver the wheelchair excessively – a maximum clear dimension of 71in is suggested.

Try out different working heights before making a final decision on work surfaces. Recommended heights are 31in for wheelchair users and 35in for ambulant disabled people. Remember, for wheelchair users, a knee recess is needed at the sink and food preparation areas – the recommended minimum height is 26in with a 24in depth.

Opinion favors a U-shaped or L-shaped kitchen with concentrated cooking, storage, and dishwashing areas. These are also useful for those with difficulty lifting and carrying, as items can be pushed along the work surface.

Planning considerations

Remember that people don't come in one size or have similar physical advantages. Consider the following points.

Appliances

▸ Electric appliances are better for those with physical challenges, as they are easier to operate. Electric ovens give off no carbon monoxide or combustibles – someone with impaired smell might not detect a gas leak.

▸ The microwave is the best appliance for the universal kitchen. It doesn't produce combustible gases, cooks quickly, and is easy and safe to operate. Plastic containers can be used, which are lighter and do not conduct heat. Talking microwaves can assist the elderly and visually impaired.

▸ Front controls mean you don't have to reach over hot burners. Electronic touch controls are easy to operate.

▸ A lift-up cooktop guard offers protection from the hot elements for children and the visually impaired.

▸ Raising the dishwasher about 10in off the floor will avoid the need to bend down and reduce back strain.

▸ Siting the oven and microwave at mid-height level is particularly useful for wheelchair users. Otherwise, smaller, tabletop version will minimize bending.

▸ Side-opening oven doors allow easier access.

▸ Go for visual contrasts so areas and controls are easier to see, which will help to prevent potential accidents. Opt for black heating elements on a white cooktop or white ceramic elements in a metal or black cooktop.

▸ Controls can be adapted with tactile or Braille markings for people with a visual impairment.

Sinks and faucets

▸ Shallow sinks are easier to reach into and provide more clearance underneath.

▸ A sink center has been developed that can be raised or lowered at will to suit the user. It is operated electronically or manually, and is perfect for households where height of user varies, or if the kitchen is shared by a chair-bound person and able-bodied family members.

▸ Single-lever faucets are easier to use for the less dexterous, especially those with a long lever that can be operated with the elbow. Electronically controlled, touch-sensitive faucets turn on by waving your hand under the spout and breaking the infrared beam.

Furniture and fixtures

▸ A roll-out cabinet on casters can be moved under the counter or out of the way when necessary.

▸ Shallow shelves insure easy access.

▸ Tall, pull-out storage cabinets and door-mounted racks allow easy access to stored items.

▸ Pull-out or fold-down kitchen tables will provide extra workspace and can retract for wheelchair passage.

▸ Wheelchair users need a space measuring 30 x 47in beside the kitchen table for eating comfortably.

ECO-FRIENDLY KITCHENS

Organic food is increasingly popular and widely available, but you should also consider the cooking environment itself. There are plenty of materials and equipment available that will create a hardwearing, stylish kitchen but also present less of a threat to the environment.

Buying reclaimed and antique furniture is a good way of cutting down on wastage. Visit reclamation yards and antiques shops and look for pieces that can be incorporated into your kitchen, such as apron sinks and reconditioned 1950s fridges. Many furniture makers will adapt old pieces to new forms and uses.

If you are buying brand-new wooden cabinets, look for companies with a responsible attitude to the environment. Choose a company that uses wood grown from sustainable sources and check for certificates of authenticity. Some may also recycle wood shavings, use scraps as firewood, and plant trees in their local community as a goodwill gesture.

Try to select materials that will last and can be easily repaired rather than ones that will have to be replaced. Wood is a good choice for countertops, particularly American and European hardwoods like oak, beech, and maple, which are strong and easy to maintain. Avoid tropical hardwoods such as teak, iroko, and wenge, unless they are bought from reclamation or salvage yards.

Flooring too is most environmentally friendly when it is made from durable materials that do not need frequent replacement. An untreated solid wood floor finished with a natural oil or wax is more ecologically sound than laminated flooring, which has a high synthetic content. Bamboo is also available as a floor and countertop and, being a grass rather than a hardwood, it is extremely fast-growing (it can grow up to 3ft a day) so plantations are quickly replenished. Stone flooring is also long lasting, although reclaimed stone is preferable to newly quarried stone, and it may have an interesting history to add to its character.

If you experience sensitivity or allergies to conventional paints, try a natural alternative. Instead of using petro-chemicals, environmentally friendly paints use linseed oil

LEFT: Reclaimed wooden countertops are solid, weighty, and hardwearing, and add an idiosyncratic charm. The look is complemented by the original wood flooring and hefty butcher block. Against plain walls, the character of such features stands out. **BELOW:** Using a modern mixture of glass and steel frame, this kitchen addition leads on to luxuriant greenery outside. The contemporary structure not only injects a huge amount of light and airiness into the room, but complements the clean lines of the limestone counter, pure white cabinets, and heavy apron sink.

and natural raw materials and can be tinted with mineral and earth pigments such as ultramarine blue and red iron oxide. Conventional paints contain volatile organic compounds (VOCs), mainly solvents, which contribute to air pollution and smog, so look out for paint ranges with a low VOC content. Many natural paints are also virtually odorless and allow you to breathe safely. In addition, you can buy natural, non-toxic wood treatments such as wax, oil, stain, and varnish for use on countertops, furniture, and floors. And keep an eye out for eco-friendly cleaning products that are biodegradable; avoid petrochemicals, synthetic fragrances, animal testing and chlorine bleaches.

Those with a garden or field would be wise to recycle a mound of general household rubbish using a bonfire and a properly built compost heap. Grass mowings, annual (but not perennial) weeds, vegetable peelings, and dead leaves can all be used to make a rich, healthy fertilizer and soil conditioner for the garden, for free. Compost heaps should be moist but not wet and protected from excessive rain, which will leach the nutrients you are trying to save.

BUILT-IN OR FREESTANDING?

Once you have the basic layout of your kitchen in place, you need to decide whether you want a built-in or "modular" approach. Smart banks of streamlined, built-in cabinets that neatly contain every one of your appliances were once the number one choice for the kitchen-buying public. But a resurgence in "modular-style" kitchens has created a division between the two approaches.

A modular, freestanding design breaks with the traditional idea of planning a kitchen around banks of built-in cabinets. Instead, the basic premise harks back to the 1950s, when kitchens were put together piece by piece. The modern version offers individual, freestanding elements, each one housing a different function: cooking modules with a cooktop and built-in oven; washing elements with sink and draining board; and preparation centers with countertop and storage space. The traditional island unit has also been given a facelift to become a sleek, laboratory-style workbench that is now often the centerpiece of the kitchen, complete with appliances and storage space. This look is chic and sophisticated. Most modules use a combination of materials such as aluminum, etched glass, and colored lacquers and stand on chiseled legs to create an airy, open feel.

If you have a smaller kitchen, it is probably best to opt for built-in cabinets where every last inch of space can be utilized with good planning and design. But modular kitchens do offer many advantages. They are incredibly flexible and you can build up your own design with different elements and create your own unique, mix-and-match style by adding an old distressed hutch or a bold retro-style fridge-freezer. It allows you to tailor your kitchen to suit your lifestyle and the look of your home.

Modular kitchens can also be bought piece by piece, so you don't have to spend a substantial amount of money immediately as you would with built-ins. You could start with a cooktop and oven unit while retaining the existing built-in

FAR LEFT: A wheeled drinks cart provides extra storage for everyday cooking utensils.
LEFT: A carefully balanced combination of permanent storage and movable cupboards breaks up the uniformity of this single-line kitchen. The steel fronts and exposed sink insure it retains an eclectic, but contemporary flavor.

ABOVE: A reconditioned 1950s oven and a wall-mounted water heater add an idiosyncratic twist to this modern kitchen. The bright, spacious room makes good use of freestanding furniture, with light flooding in though the full-length windows.
RIGHT: Translucent glass, shiny metal, and white walls keep this modular kitchen open and airy.

LEFT: The mixture of built-in cabinets and sculptural workbench on legs is the key to this efficient, streamlined workspace. The clean lines are echoed by two uninterrupted shelves, stacked with neat piles of white crockery and glassware and a wall of clear glass windows. **BELOW:** Classic, Shaker-style cabinets are smartly offset by an industrial cook center and a butcher block on casters. **BELOW RIGHT:** Flexible kitchen design makes sense in a one-space home such as this. The island unit is made of two wheeled cabinets with raised edges along the back and sides, so the food preparation is not on full view when facing those in the living area. The units can be wheeled closer to the appliances when cooking or moved out of the way when not in use.

cabinets, and add more as funds permit and your plans develop. Perhaps best of all, a modular kitchen is also a portable kitchen, so you can simply pack it up and take it all with you when you move homes. With this in mind, it is probably worth investing in good-quality pieces that will stand the test of time.

The choice rests mainly on taste and in reality most kitchens contain both built-in and freestanding elements.

Modular appliances

In the last few years, freestanding kitchen appliances have been transformed into big, beautiful "focus" machines. From the larger-than-life fridge-freezer, to the cool, aluminum dishwasher and the range in all its guises, these are appliances that make a statement as soon as you walk into the kitchen. They can be used to great effect to break up a line of uniform built-in cabinets and add a striking edge to an otherwise ordinary kitchen.

The natural progression of this trend is the introduction of "modular" appliance units. These stand-alone modules take built-in appliances out of built-in cabinets and house them in tall freestanding frames or columns. Each module can include one or two kitchen functions, say a microwave and a fridge, or an oven and a dishwasher. They can be used individually as freestanding elements or can be integrated into your existing kitchen.

The look takes its cue from the professional kitchen – units are angular, sleek, and usually made from stainless steel. There are also low-level modules with sinks and cooktops to complete the deconstructed look. This piece-by-piece approach allows you to build up your kitchen as you like and offers numerous layout possibilities. The key is flexibility, but make sure you take time and seek advice when planning this type of kitchen – modular units do not use space as efficiently as a built-in kitchen.

ABOVE RIGHT: The single line of cabinets is echoed by the rectangular dining table, which is close enough to enable hot food to be served quickly to diners. **BOTTOM LEFT:** The built-in kitchen takes on a whole new meaning with this "kitchen-in-a-box" design, where appliances and gadgets can be hidden away. **BOTTOM RIGHT:** This kitchen exploits the corner space of an open-plan mezzanine. The combination of steel fronts and pale wood is unobtrusive but modern. **RIGHT:** An island unit is a good way of subtly blurring the boundaries between eating and dining while retaining a feeling of openness. A sweeping apex ceiling with exposed beams is the perfect foil to this neat built-in kitchen.

case study: THE COMBINATION KITCHEN

Combining built-in contemporary elements with freestanding traditional pieces, the kitchen in this Manhattan loft provides a hospitable place for cooking and entertaining. When Jan Hashey and Yasuo Minagawa commissioned architect Deborah Berke to come up with a design, the entire space was raw, with concrete ceilings, walls, and floors. Her robust approach was to use a palette of simple materials and ready-made cabinets to complement the clients' collection of salvaged and flea-market finds. Although the rest of the loft has a more minimal quality, maximizing the sense of space, the clients wanted the kitchen to be a place where they could display their collection of Japanese pots and crockery and entertain guests while cooking. Directly leading from the kitchen is an open dining area.

FAR LEFT: The centerpiece of the layout is an old marble-topped kitchen table with turned legs, which originally came from the area around the couple's upstate weekend home. Although the table is not valuable, it is very fragile and had to be shipped as an art object to prevent damage in transit. A steel rail provides hanging space for pots and pans over a huge 8-ring steel range; the double-door stainless steel fridge is built in. Flooring is extra-wide wood planks; exposing the feet of the built-in cabinets enhances the feeling of space. **LEFT:** The counter, with its integral backsplash, is made of concrete; cabinetry is in maple. The wall-mounted wooden storage unit provides a place to display a collection of Japanese pots and crockery.

ESSENTIAL SERVICES

When altering or installing services such as electricity, gas, and water, you must employ a professional electrician and plumber. Find them either by personal recommendation (your kitchen company, friends, or relatives) or by contacting professional trade bodies. These professional bodies should be able to give you a list of reputable members and may offer guarantees and insurance against negligence.

It is crucial that work is coordinated when employing different professionals. For instance, call in a plumber before the subfloor, insulation, plastering, and plasterboard are installed. Also, plan as far in advance as possible and decide which appliances you are likely to need in your new kitchen, even those you want at a later date, so that the installation of supply and waste pipes and electrical wiring can be achieved in one simple and economical operation.

Plumbing

Your kitchen may only require water pipes to the sink and dishwasher and a gas supply to the oven. However, brief the plumber if you want a garbage disposer, hot-water dispenser, or water purification system, for example.

Cold-water drinking faucets should branch directly off the incoming water supply and not the storage tank. Different regions have different water. If your water leaves a bad taste in your mouth or is foul-smelling, a water-purification system is the best antidote. This has a carbon filter to trap sediment and combat odors. Hard water can cause many problems; mineral salts cause scale build-up on electric heating elements and inside hot-water heaters and radiators. In addition, soap will be difficult to lather and sinks will have stubborn scum marks. A whole-house water softener can prevent the damaging effects of hard water by converting these salts into sodium salts, which do no harm. It should be connected into the incoming water supply after the branch to the kitchen cold faucet since it is actually healthier to drink hard water than soft.

Drains from sinks and garbage disposers should be fitted with a trap to prevent unpleasant odors from coming back into the room and to provide an easily accessible stop valve so any blockages can be cleared from the drainpipe.

Lead pipes carry a serious health hazard. If your house or apartment contains lead pipes, try to negotiate with your plumber. Some will waive installation fees and install replacement pipes for free because the lead ones can be sold as scrap to salvage yards.

Gas

Because of its explosive nature, natural gas should only be installed by a qualified professional. Consult a professionally registered tradesman before you move gas appliances and when you have a new gas range, oven, or cooktop installed.

Electricity

The electricity supply in your kitchen should always be earthed to prevent appliances from becoming live. Insure that there are plenty of accessible outlets, that equipment is in good repair, and there are no trailing or frayed cords. If you have just moved, especially into an older building, or are rewiring your kitchen or installing new outlets, have the electrical system tested by a registered electrician. Look for a professional body whose duty it is to protect consumers against the hazards of unsafe and unsound electrical installations. It can supply a list of approved, technically competent contractors, plus a formal, established complaints procedure should the work not be carried out to high enough standards. It is always best to employ a professional electrician to install outlets as well as high-wattage appliances such as ranges and water heaters.

If you are planning from scratch, think about your lighting scheme – whether or not you want dimmers, two-way switches, track lighting, or recessed lighting. The challenge is to build electric outlets into your plan before the electrician begins installation and before walls, tiles, or backsplashes are in place. You should also have a minimum of four outlets for portable electric appliances such as food processers and toasters, located near the spots where they are kept and away from running water.

Heating

Even though a little warmth is generated by cooking, you are likely to need an effective heating system. Wet systems use a boiler to heat water, which is then circulated through pipes into radiators. Modern boilers are becoming smaller and more efficient – some wall-mounted ones fit neatly inside a kitchen cupboard and blend in with the cabinets. Combination boilers heat cold water directly from the incoming water supply when you turn on the faucet, so you don't need a hot-water storage cylinder or a cold-water tank in your attic.

Radiators are now available in a wide range of materials, colors, shapes, and sizes to suit the style and architecture of your kitchen. There are classic, cast-iron column radiators, industrial, low-level tubes, and multifunction wall panels. Glass panel heaters are sleek and chic, and they produce an even heat by fusing a transparent electrical element between two sheets of glass. Kick-plate convector heaters fit discreetly into the base of kitchen cabinets and usually have a "fan-only" setting for hot weather. They free wall space in a small kitchen. Look out for dual-fuel radiators and convectors that can be powered by electricity, so you can get instant warmth even when the central heating is switched off. There are also electric-only models, which are ideal if access to pipework is difficult.

Underfloor heating is unobtrusive and creates an even temperature. It usually runs off wet systems, circulating hot water through thermoplastic pipes set in concrete, or an underfloor cavity. If you opt for an electric version, a special heating mat is laid on the floor and covered with a self-leveling compound. When set, the floor can be tiled over as normal. Underfloor heating works under any flooring material – and is particularly welcome under stone – but it can be expensive to install.

If your house is heated by a warm-air system, you can easily run a duct into the kitchen and fit a grille. However, warm-air heating can stir up dust and pollen.

Combined cooking/heating ranges run on gas, oil, or solid fuel and not only heat the kitchen, but also provide hot water and central heating for radiators around the house.

WHERE TO BUY?

Remodeling a kitchen is probably one of the most expensive improvements you're ever likely to make to your house and something you will only have to do perhaps two or three times in your lifetime. It can also be one of the most bewildering experiences if you don't know where to go, what to ask, and what to expect. Good research is therefore paramount and will help you find the kitchen that is perfect for you, your family, your house, and your budget.

There are three main ways to remodel a kitchen and, to a large extent, which you choose will depend on how much money you wish to spend. Usually the more expensive the project, the better level of service and better quality furniture and fixtures you should receive. However, even if you are buying ready-to-assemble cabinets, you should still be able to avoid substandard goods, shoddy workmanship, and poor service. All kitchen cabinet manufacturers have to meet rigorous standards set by the industry and you could also investigate warranties that cover you against defective materials or workmanship.

FAR LEFT: This larger-than-life extractor fan extends over the entire length of the island. A brave design move, it adds an unexpected industrial element to what is a modern version of the country kitchen. **LEFT:** The preparation area here is made up of everyday utility ware. Ordinary adjustable glass shelving and a plain white countertop are offset by a map of the world used as wallpaper. A length of tough, yachting rubber pulls across to conceal storage beneath. **ABOVE:** The emphasis in this kitchen is on inexpensive efficiency, practical good looks, and hardwearing materials.

Do-it-yourself

Don't be put off by the do-it-yourself label. These days large stores offer a huge range of styles and design options that echo those at the top end of the market, from cool, contemporary to the more traditional, country look. Most also offer good-quality, brand-name appliances plus sinks, faucets, counters, lighting, and flooring.

A free design service is usually available although you may need to take your own measurements into the store, as site visits aren't always on offer. Don't forget to inquire about computer-aided design so you can see your kitchen as a color, 3-D plan and then receive a printout to take home with you to examine at leisure.

Do-it-yourself cabinets are likely to be of the flat-pack variety for home assembly, although certain stores do offer the option of a rigid, factory-assembled version. Unless you are a trained kitchen fitter or an accomplished amateur, it is wise to call in the professionals. Most do-it-yourself chains have an in-house installation service or can recommend fitters in your area. Don't forget to ask for a written quotation for the installation service before you agree. While the price of the kitchen may seem good value for money, extra charges, such as installation and delivery, can easily double the total cost of a new kitchen. Also check what kind of after-sales service the store offers including helplines and insurance-backed guarantees.

The kitchen showroom

If you have a larger budget available, an independent kitchen showroom will offer a large selection of brands including German, Italian, and French cabinets. Most showrooms will be able to work within a set budget so don't be put off by pricey-looking window displays. They should also offer the same level of service to each customer regardless of how much the kitchen costs.

The kitchen showroom should be able to take care of the whole job for you – from ripping out your old cabinets to installing lighting, flooring, appliances, and new cabinets. Ask questions and establish what the service includes – for example, home visits and planning. Nearly all showrooms require a deposit of some kind, but the amount they charge can vary dramatically. As a guide, expect to pay around 25 percent of the total cost.

The custom kitchen

This is the haute couture of the kitchen world, a design tailormade to suit your ideas, needs, and space. A kitchen designer will begin by showing you examples of his designs, then discuss colors, materials, and finishes to create a one-off kitchen. This will inevitably require a lot of input from you at the design stage, so make sure you have a fairly firm but not inflexible idea of what you want from your kitchen before you make any appointments.

To a degree, every custom-kitchen manufacturer will specialize in a certain style of kitchen, so avoid the company that is known for its rustic, country look if you want a sleek, modern design. As with any one-to-one service, expect to pay a premium for a custom kitchen, so advise them of your budget before you begin work. However, that's not to say this type of kitchen is completely out of your price bracket even if you are working within a restricted budget. Once the designer has presented you with a plan, you could ask about replacing some of the more expensive materials with cheaper alternatives to keep costs down. For example, you might substitute wood veneer for solid wood cabinets, or a good-quality laminate for granite countertops.

As custom-kitchen companies offer such a personal, one-to-one service, you are likely to form a very good working relationship with your designer, and the after-sales service is usually second to none.

Questions to ask

What does the price include? Make sure you get a detailed quotation that covers every aspect of the job including fitting, tiling, flooring, and any structural alterations you have discussed. Only when you have received an overall price for everything you have asked for, will you be able to make a fair comparison with other quotes.

Is there a free design service? Most showrooms offer this as a free service but check to see that an extra charge isn't added on to your total bill. Some designers will charge you for plans because they are extremely detailed and can include hand-drawn and computer-designed images.

How long will the job take? Ask how long the kitchen will take to arrive and how long the fitting will take – for extra reassurance, get a written estimate. Be prepared to wait some weeks, especially if the kitchen has to be ordered from abroad, if it is an unusual size or specification, or if you are having made-to-order features.

How strong is the kitchen? Ask what the doors are made of and how sturdy the furniture is. Unless you go for a custom kitchen, the carcases will usually be made from melamine-covered particleboard or medium-density fiberboard. These will vary in thickness depending on quality – from 1in at the budget end of the market up to 1¼in for a mid-range kitchen. Custom kitchens may have medium-density fiberboard carcases faced with a matching veneer. Check drawers and hinges and, if possible, choose metal as opposed to plastic. Insure that the lower cabinets are firm – a piece of particleboard stapled to the frame won't last, and if the cabinets are in medium-density fiberboard, check that it is water-resistant; particleboard isn't.

Installation

Once you have decided on the final layout of your new kitchen, it is time to call in the professionals, unless you are an expert fitter yourself. Get at least three written quotes from builders, kitchen fitters, plumbers, and electricians so that you can compare their prices. As with most matters, recommendation is a good start. If a friend, relative, or colleague has had a kitchen remodeled recently, ask which fitters they used and what they thought of them. The company you are buying your cabinets from may have their own team of in-house fitters or else a recommended list who are skilled and trustworthy tradespeople.

There are four basic phases to remodeling a kitchen: structure, services, finishes, and fixtures, and then there is the equipment. After you have settled on a kitchen plan, the first thing that must be done is structural work. If there is damp, it must be treated. Then wiring, plumbing, and gas installation must be completed. When the shell (the room itself) is finished, the fixtures, equipment, and appliances can be introduced. The key is to plan in a logical order. For instance, electrical wiring for lights and wall outlets should be done before plastering and tiling; appliances ideally should be installed after flooring is laid.

If building work is going on at the same time, the new cabinets should be delivered only when construction is complete and the room is ready. Most companies need to be satisfied that the kitchen will not be damaged by prevailing site conditions, such as new plaster, or used by other tradespeople working at the premises. To promote good teamwork, introduce the different tradespeople to each other and make sure they understand each other's requirements. Ask for a schedule of work from everyone involved so you can monitor each stage as it progresses. If building work runs over and your kitchen cannot be delivered on the agreed fit date, check that it can be stored for no extra cost.

There are three different types of "fit." A "dry fit" includes installing furniture and appliances, but not making the final connections of the appliances. Any waste generated by the kitchen installation is removed but the price does not include stripping out existing furniture. A "wet fit" is the same as a dry fit but also includes all plumbing and electrical connections, while a "turn-key" operation is a combination of dry and wet fits plus all finishes including paintwork and flooring; in other words, the complete job.

After the job is finished, allocate a drawer or dedicated space to keep all the information about the maintenance of your kitchen cabinets, counters, tiles, and flooring. Start a file and include maintenance manuals for your equipment and appliances, plus guarantees and servicing documents. A tool kit can also prove indispensable in the kitchen.

Once you have considered the basics of planning, determined the best layout for your kitchen, and, crucially, decided where it should be located with respect to other areas in the home, you can begin to think about the kitchen as a space or room in its own right. As with any other part of the home, this partly entails exploring issues to do with color, pattern, and texture, basic elements that comprise the decorative palette. But in this context it is equally important to pay attention to those individual or idiosyncratic touches that express a sense of character and personality. The preferences you express elsewhere in your home shouldn't stop short at the kitchen door.

Kitchen Living

The idea of the kitchen as a space worthy of decorative consideration would have vastly entertained our great-grandparents, for whom the kitchen was the largely unseen engine room behind the green baize door. As long as kitchens remained the domain of servants, there was no question of fitting, furnishing, or decorating them with anything in mind beyond practical utility. Of course, many such kitchens, particularly those extensive service areas "below stairs" found in the great country houses, have their own elemental appeal; I have always particularly admired the scrubbed simplicity of traditional larders, stillrooms, pantries, and dairies. But in most households, the kitchen was generally a fairly inhospitable place, badly lit, poorly ventilated, and soberly decorated in order to disguise the discoloration caused by coal-fired stoves and gas lighting.

After the successive social upheavals following two world wars, when the average kitchen had become a one-person, or more accurately, one-woman operation, huge emphasis was placed on efficiency and ergonomics. Inspired by built-in kitchen designs originally developed in the 1920s, and equipped with the latest labor-saving appliances, many postwar kitchens resembled nothing so much as miniature domestic production lines, clad in new easy-clean laminates, floored in the ubiquitous linoleum or vinyl, and lit with flickering fluorescent tubes.

Reaction to the sterility of these environments, combined with a growing informality of lifestyle from the 1960s onward, led to the kitchen being dressed up in any number of styles: townhouses had their "country" kitchens; the latest modern appliances were concealed behind turn-of-the-century-style panels; acres of stainless steel elevated the home cook to the food technician.

Today, kitchens no longer have a point to prove. The fully built-in custom kitchen is still a status symbol and there are plenty of people who are prepared to invest huge sums of money to make that kind of statement. But a more relaxed

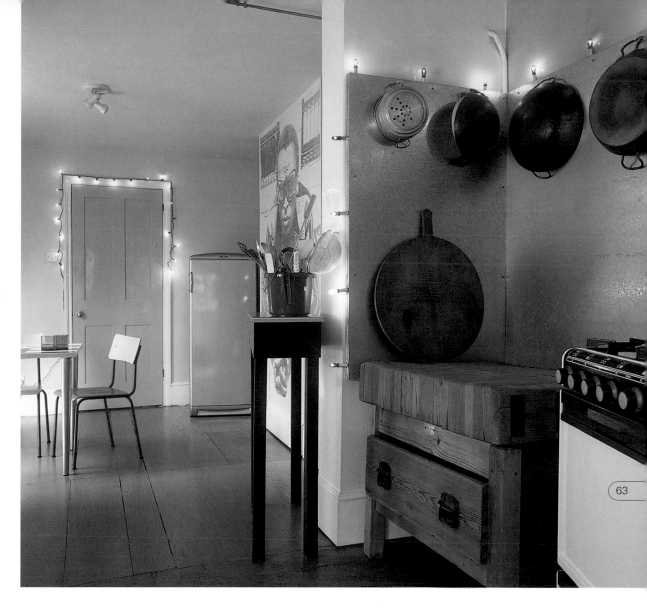

LEFT: A glazed ceiling bathes a kitchen area in natural light, providing optimum conditions for cooking. An indoor swing reflects the easy informality of this airy open-plan space.
RIGHT: Colored Christmas tree lights add a quirky personal touch to a kitchen-diner, simply furnished with freestanding appliances and fixtures, including an old butcher block.

approach is becoming increasingly popular, where old and new, built-in and freestanding elements work happily together. This is not to say that kitchen "style" is now an irrelevance, rather that people are beginning to accept that it can emerge partly through personal taste, partly as a response to context and, crucially, as an expression of the way they want to live.

Accordingly, instead of presenting a range of kitchen "styles," this chapter is organized according to different patterns of kitchen use. The sections are not intended to be watertight, merely to distill some common themes that inform design and decoration. Although the type of kitchen that would suit a busy professional is unlikely to be adequate for a family with young children, distinctions are not always so clearcut and you may well find yourself picking different elements to suit your own surroundings and needs.

An obvious parameter for most people is the amount of space they have at their disposal. But as the previous chapter on planning has demonstrated, a small kitchen does not mean that you should restrain your ideas; spatial limitations can often be overcome by clever planning, both of the notional kitchen space and of the home as a whole.

Space is a critical issue, but it can be just as important to spend some time thinking about how you like to cook and by extension how you like to live. You don't necessarily have to have a hungry family to cater for to benefit from an inclusive kitchen, for example – this pattern would also suit single people who like to entertain. Those wedded to traditional methods of cooking or those with a taste for robust simplicity might equally appreciate the elemental qualities of a vernacular kitchen. While keen gardeners are obvious candidates for kitchens that merge with outdoor spaces, many people relish any opportunity to move outside, weather permitting.

Successful kitchens are founded on careful planning; kitchens where you want to spend time are those that reflect how you live.

LEFT: Intense shades are increasingly seen in the kitchen. Deep orange walls create a lively and hospitable background. "White goods," the old term for household appliances, are now available in a range of strong accent colors. **ABOVE:** Here, color accentuates spatial planning, adding a welcome level of interest to a sleek fitted area.

LEFT AND BELOW: A space-age update of the old serving hatch, this extra-deep opening, within a built-in storage wall, provides a visual link between kitchen and eating area, allowing natural light to penetrate the kitchen. The glossy finish on the cabinets was achieved with five coats of polyurethane.

BELOW RIGHT: A simple run of white kitchen cabinets with a stainless steel backsplash is lifted out of the ordinary by a playful approach to decoration. Kitchens are now increasingly emerging as living areas in their own right, a trend that has been signaled by a heightened interest in colors and finishes.

Decorative choices

Even the most cursory glance through a pile of brochures from manufacturers, dealers, and retailers is enough to indicate the huge breadth of choice facing consumers today. Where safe neutral shades, uniformly white appliances, and smooth synthetic textures once used to predominate, there has been something of a decorative explosion.

This breadth of choice is particularly evident when it comes to color. White, with its connotations of purity, hygiene, and freshness, has always had a strong association

with kitchens. Perhaps it all goes back to that familiar combination of white and blue which was such a feature of traditional dairies and stillrooms (blue was believed to act as a fly-repellent). With the emergence of the built-in kitchen in the early decades of the twentieth century, white was widely adopted as a hallmark of domestic efficiency and good housekeeping; it's not surprising that household appliances are popularly termed "white goods."

Similarly, the country kitchen aesthetic accounts for the long-standing popularity of neutral decorative schemes. Buffs, creams, browns, terra-cottas, and off-whites are the natural partners of kitchen schemes featuring surfaces made of wood, brick, stone, and tile.

In recent years, however, the kitchen has shrugged off its neutral image and embraced strong color, a change that signals the transformation of the kitchen from behind-the-scenes workroom to living area in its own right. Where kitchen color was once restricted to those incidental accents provided by enameled saucepans for example, or a platter of fresh fruit or vegetables, it is increasingly employed in a more positive and deliberate fashion to define space, enhance light, and generate mood and atmosphere. White goods themselves are white no longer, but available in every conceivable shade from navy blue to shocking pink, as much a part of the design scheme as a working appliance.

In the kitchen, as in any interior, color can be used to enhance the effect of natural light. Light, airy backgrounds make a space seem brighter and more spacious; warmer,

FAR LEFT TOP: "Bookworm," Ron Arad's innovative approach to shelving, complements the sleek curve of the kitchen counter. **FAR LEFT BOTTOM:** A blue rubber floor demarcates a kitchen area, a material shift that is about practicality as much as aesthetics. The neat coverstrip between the kitchen flooring and the natural fiber carpet in the main living area is a key detail here. **LEFT:** Color can be immensely uplifting; even small touches of color create a positive effect. A single wall picked out in a warm red serves as a vivid backdrop for the display of children's artwork.

richer tones provide a cozy sense of enclosure. At the same time, vibrant planes of color, picking out a single wall or horizontal surface, serve to delineate space, which can be particularly valuable in an open-plan, multipurpose area. A robust and confident use of color also helps to generate a sense of vitality, even personality, signaling the kitchen's wider role as living area.

In many ways, texture is just as important as color and in some instances can even stand in for it. Cooking, in its proper sense (that is, when it is not merely a question of setting the microwave), is an activity that relies heavily on touch and feel. The "hands-on" nature of kitchen work only goes to heighten our awareness of texture in the surfaces with which we regularly come into contact. For this reason, seamless kitchens where surfaces are uniformly smooth can be rather uneasy, characterless places and serve to undermine our enjoyment and appreciation of food with all our senses.

The more subdued the colors, the greater the emphasis on texture should be to provide a sense of character and depth. Highly reflective surfaces, such as stainless steel, glass, and glazed ceramic tiles, add a sparkling crispness to a decorative scheme. Matte surfaces such as wood and certain types of stone provide a subtle tactility. In many cases, textural variety is a natural outcome of material choice. A scheme that features different materials used as flooring, on work surfaces, or on the walls will often have inbuilt textural character.

Synthetics have their place in kitchen design, and new types of plastic, particularly lighter and more translucent forms of polypropylene, are vast improvements on dreary postwar artificial materials. But in the context of texture, natural materials will always have the edge, simply because they age so well and have the potential to improve with wear and sympathetic maintenance. Battered plastic or scratched laminate utterly lacks the charm of a wooden surface that has been subjected to the same treatment.

Where there is textural character, inevitably there is also pattern: the flecked surface of granite, the grain of wood, and the gridded appearance of tile and mosaic are all patterns of a sort. What is infinitely less successful and

RIGHT: Light, both natural and artificial, adds vitality to neutral surroundings. In this all-white kitchen, light from a skylight is supplemented by spotlights over the counter and a large photographer's spot that illuminates the living area. **INSET RIGHT:** Material quality speaks for itself. A pale stone counter complements the stone tiled flooring, which extends to the outdoor area. **FAR RIGHT:** A luminous effect has been achieved by painting a wooden floor white and tiling kitchen surfaces in gray mosaic. The dining table is a white painted medium-density fiberboard top over a steel base.

ABOVE A subtle combination of materials, from painted to natural wood, stainless steel to mosaic, provides inherent depth of character that complements the mixture of traditional elements, such as the apron sink, and more contemporary detailing. **BELOW:** A portion of wall painted with latex chalkboard paint provides a handy space for messages and reminders, and a good alternative to a noticeboard. **RIGHT:** A stainless steel work surface and appliances are set off by Op Art-inspired patterns that have been laminated onto a dining table and cabinet fronts. The upper and lower cabinets are uniform to emphasize the graphic nature of the scheme.

utterly depressing is where pattern is used to 'prettify' or somehow distract one's attention away from the essentially utilitarian or practical nature of the kitchen. Decorative motifs on teakettles and toasters, stenciled drawer fronts, even patterned paper kitchen towels are all examples of this meretricious use of pattern to embellish what ought to be allowed to speak for itself. More sympathetic in the kitchen context, however, are retro patterns from the 1950s or 1960s, which can add a quirky, tongue-in-cheek quality...if used sparingly!

Pattern adds vitality, movement, and rhythm to the interior. In this sense, it is less about superfluous decorative flourishes and more about arrangement. A row of spice jars, bottles of oils, vinegars, and wines, beautiful graphics on food packaging, a random collection of fridge magnets, an appetizing display of fresh fruit and vegetables, or a sculptural array of cooking utensils are all natural kitchen patterns that delight the eye.

case study: KITCHEN COLOR

Color is uniquely uplifting, but it is also a good way of delineating space. In this open-plan living/working/eating space in London, a singing shade of bright yellow defines a kitchen area. The single-level house was designed in 1968 by the celebrated architect Richard Rogers, for his mother. Today, it is the home of Rogers's son, Ab, his partner, Sophie Braimbridge, and their daughter, Ella. Both Ab, who is a furniture designer, and Sophie, a chef and food writer, work from home and the inclusivity of the space is a positive bonus. A unifying feature is the glossy epoxy resin flooring, which, like the bold color scheme, has remained unchanged since the house was first designed.

LEFT: The yellow island runs almost the whole length of the space. On the "living" side it is fully built-in, with capacious cupboards. **ABOVE:** On the "kitchen" side, the island houses the working elements, with the preparation area tidily concealed behind an upstand. Faucets are mounted directly on the upstand to make full use of the space, with pipes and wiring routed through the internal structure of the island. Along with a wood-fired pizza oven in the backyard, the kitchen provides the perfect place for Sophie to test recipes and plan cooking courses. Ab's computer workstation is set up to one side of the dining area, away from kitchen noise.

THE INCLUSIVE KITCHEN

Embracing a wide range of household activities, many of which may have little to do with either cooking or eating, the inclusive kitchen is a flexible pattern that has become increasingly popular in recent years. This particular category includes kitchen-diners, multipurpose cooking/eating/living areas, and large family kitchens that act as a nerve center for the entire household.

Like many trends in interior design, the inclusive kitchen is not so much a new idea as an old idea newly discovered. Centuries before houses were subdivided into rooms, each with its own assigned function, the hall house of the Middle Ages was basically a single enclosed space. Around its central hearth, all the activities of the household took place, the most critical being cooking and eating.

Of course, the inclusive kitchen does not represent an attempt to turn back the clock to a medieval lifestyle, or even a conscious reinvention of this ancient pattern. But it does imply a similar lack of hierarchy in the way domestic life is organized and an absence of the distinction between what goes on behind the scenes and what is open to view.

The central feature of the inclusive kitchen is a certain generosity of spirit. It's a place where everyone can join in together to prepare a meal, sit down to eat it, and clear up afterward. It's where children can absorb some of the basic skills involved in cooking through sheer proximity to the main focus of activity; and where parents can keep an eye on youngsters playing or doing their homework. It's somewhere friends and visitors can drop by and instantly feel welcome. Inevitably, in households where there are pets, it's also where you'll find the dog basket or the cat curled up in a patch of sun.

If it is generous in spirit, the inclusive kitchen need not necessarily occupy vast amounts of floor area. Paradoxically, this particular pattern often works just as well where space is limited as it does when there is plenty of room to play around with. If you're short of space, the kitchen per se can be no more than a compact functional zone slotted into a general living area. One of the advantages of this arrangement is that it combines a feeling of spaciousness with the ease of operation that results when kitchens are tightly planned.

LEFT: Generous in spirit and size, true industrial-scale lofts provide the perfect setting for the inclusive kitchen. Here the cooking area occupies a corner of the space, with a run of cabinets serving as a divider.

ABOVE: Another counter-cum-divider demarcates space in an open-plan living/eating/cooking area. With all the fixtures concealed, the kitchen virtually disappears from view when not in use.

Defining areas

Inclusive kitchens have few physical barriers to separate them from other areas in the home. Decoratively speaking, it is therefore important for the space to read as a coherent whole. One way of achieving this is to use the same colors or materials throughout, so that the planes of walls, ceiling, and floor provide a unified backdrop.

At the same time, a multipurpose space often benefits from a decorative strategy that draws some distinction between different areas. Accents of strong color can be used to define areas within the space or suggest a boundary between one area and another. For example, picking out a wall next to a dining table in a vivid shade provides a focus for eating, while a bright kitchen counter can serve as a visual marker between the relaxing or living side of the space and the practical, working side.

More subtle signals can be sent out in the form of changes in materials. It often makes sense to vary materials in an open-plan area, particularly those used for flooring, to address different practical requirements. Where a kitchen area might require the easy maintenance of tiles, linoleum,

resin, or similar surfaces, you may wish to provide more comfort underfoot in the the space set aside for eating or relaxation. Varying the material but sticking to the same overall color or tone is the most understated approach, but a decorative shift of gear can be very effective, too, especially in a larger space.

The shape of the room and any existing architectural features can also be useful for adding a sense of definition. L-shaped layouts offer a natural break between activities; alcoves, recesses, and redundant chimney breasts can be exploited to create areas for built-in kitchen storage. Any change in level, however minor – a step up or down – can also be used to demarcate different areas. Otherwise, you could always manufacture a change in level by constructing a platform to raise the kitchen area up slightly.

The inclusive kitchen means that, for at least some of the time, cooking is going to be an activity carried out in public view. As a result, a degree of separation, no matter how minimal, between functional areas and relaxing or eating areas, is important from both a practical and a psychological point of view. If you're a nervous or tentative

FAR LEFT: An open stairway, with a sleek metal banister supported on fine steel cabling, separates the cooking and eating end of the room from the main living area. Good-looking modular storage organizes clutter in a working wall.
LEFT: Double-height spaces offer alternative ways of defining areas. A room within a room, this kitchen is partly concealed behind a high counter that serves to screen work in progress without isolating the cook.

cook, it helps if every faltering attempt to follow a recipe isn't open to scrutiny. But even if you're a confident show-off, some kind of barrier between the cooking area and the rest of the space can be a useful aid to concentration. Cooking often means working in extreme conditions, in close proximity to searing heat, steam, sharp knives, and heavy pans. Whatever helps you to focus on the task in hand is a positive asset.

At the same time, unless you are an exceptionally tidy cook, or you scrupulously wash each dirty dish as you go along, kitchen clutter and the detritus that inevitably results from the production of a meal are going to be something of an eyesore for those sitting down to enjoy that meal or relaxing afterward. There will be times, in a multipurpose space, when you want to forget that the kitchen is there.

A counter with a raised upstand serving to conceal both kitchen debris and the cook's every move is one solution to this problem. An alternative is to locate the kitchen area along the length of a wall, with sliding doors or folding screens that close off the space when it is not in use. Open shelf units also make good spatial dividers without screening off the kitchen area entirely, and are ideal for displaying kitchenalia. Translucent panels running from floor to ceiling can screen kitchen clutter without blocking light; if they are folding or sliding you can keep your options open.

Practicalities

The inclusive kitchen can present something of a practical challenge. It's all very well to plan your multipurpose space so that it functions as one smooth flow of activity from area to area, where meals are prepared and whisked immediately

LEFT: A strategic use of color highlights different areas of activity within an open space. A robust freestanding partition partially encloses the kitchen area and screens the cooktops. Seamless detailing and well-judged proportions contribute to the success of the result.
BELOW FAR LEFT: Simple but effective apportioning of space creates separate zones for cooking, eating, and sleeping within a single area.
BELOW LEFT: A cozier version of the inclusive kitchen features copper-bottomed pans over a traditional range, a dining table fashioned from rough planks, and tailored kitchen storage.

Another key practicality is lighting. In the inclusive kitchen, flexibility is essential. Preparation areas, counters, sinks, and cooktops need good task lighting so that chopping, cutting, and handling sizzling or simmering pans can be carried out safely. Because the level of lighting required for these practical chores is generally higher and more directional in its effect than the type of lighting that is preferable for the sociable activities of eating and relaxing, it is a good idea to have the kitchen lights on a dimmer switch. That way, you can lower the light levels in the kitchen area when it's time to put food on the table.

An inclusive kitchen, where everyone is welcome, needs some extra consideration when it comes to safety. If very young children or babies are going to be playing in the kitchen – and messing about on the floor with pots and pans and bits of dried pasta has to be one of the top games of toddlerhood – make sure they are not unnecessarily exposed to hazards. Keep cords well out of reach, turn pan handles away from the edge of the cooktop, store powerful and toxic cleansers and household chemicals in a lockable cupboard, and install ovens at eye level rather than under counters to prevent accidental burns on hot doors. It's not a bad idea to keep a properly stocked first-aid box on hand in the kitchen, either.

When children play in the kitchen or when they get old enough to tackle their homework on the kitchen table, it makes sense to allocate some storage space for these activities within the kitchen. A cupboard, a lidded box, or storage space under banquettes or window seats can provide stowing space for toys, creative materials, and games. Dictionaries and reference books can be shelved along with the cookbooks.

Inclusive kitchens inevitably serve as household nerve centers. Keep a step ahead of the game by providing a place where all those vital details – everything from the phone number of the emergency plumber to the rehearsal dates for the school play – can be readily located. A bulletin board, a portion of wall painted with latex chalkboard paint, or an in-tray by the phone would work well.

to the table. But if that meal is then accompanied by the chugging of the washing machine, or if a thick fug of cooking fumes lingers long into the evening, you haven't thought everything through properly.

All kitchens require good systems of extraction, but in the case of the inclusive kitchen this requirement is particularly acute. Cooking can be a hot, humid activity, generating steam and greasy vapors. While the aroma of food cooking may well be appetizing just before you sit down to eat, stale cooking odors can be very off-putting the rest of the time. Invest in a decent cooktop hood and try to arrange the kitchen area so that it benefits from cross ventilation from opening windows or doors.

It can also be a good idea to exclude some of the noisier appliances from the kitchen itself. Washing machines and dryers are often a feature of kitchen layouts, but they can equally and just as conveniently be installed in an adjacent utility room or even in a bathroom, creating a more peaceful atmosphere in the kitchen.

FAR LEFT: Where there is sufficient ceiling height, raising a kitchen area up a step or two is an effective means of signaling a change of activity. In this serene, light-filled space the kitchen is set on a platform accessed by two shallow steps.

LEFT: A change in level has also been employed in this attic conversion to segregate the cooking and eating area from the general living space. It is important to make the change in level significant enough to avoid the risk of tripping.

THE SMALL KITCHEN

If most people's idea of a dream kitchen tends to be somewhere that is large and open, you might well assume that a small kitchen isn't something you would choose, but something you get forced into by circumstances. Certainly, small kitchens are frequently synonymous with a general shortage of space all around – first-time home-owners, for example, often find themselves having to compromise in this department. But not everyone wants or needs a capacious kitchen. If you are at that stage in life where you eat out regularly, or if you simply don't enjoy cooking very much, it makes far better sense to allocate less space to the kitchen and keep everything as simple and straightforward as you can.

Some people, however, serious cooks among them, actively prefer small kitchens, arguing that they make better and more efficient workspaces. There is an element of truth in this. If you have ever spent time in a professional kitchen, you will have noticed that chefs hardly ever move from the spot. Whatever they need is right at hand, or there is someone to hand it to them. When a restaurant kitchen is in full swing and the tables are packed with hungry customers, chefs need to be able to concentrate their efforts at the stove and waste as little time and energy as possible trotting to and fro. A small, well-organized kitchen can offer the same degree of control.

These observations are backed up by the ergonomic studies of kitchen activity described on page 27. First carried out in the early 1950s, the research suggests that the optimum distance between the three points of the "work

LEFT: In small kitchens, tight planning and careful design are essential to accommodate all the fixtures. Here wall-hung lockers store the bulk of kitchen paraphernalia, while a hanging rack keeps frequently used items readily at hand.

ABOVE RIGHT: A complete kitchen is concealed within a custom-designed cabinet with folding doors. **BELOW RIGHT:** Restricting the layout to one wall frees up enough space for a small table, which can double as an additional work surface.

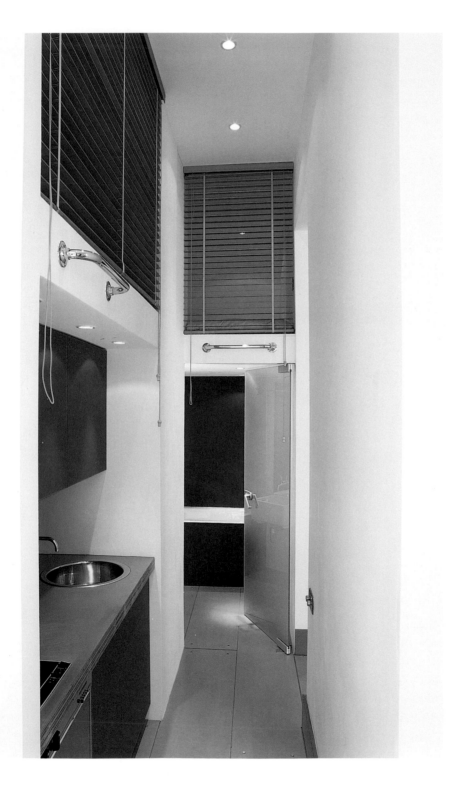

LEFT: Kitchens don't come much more compact than this narrow fitted space. Steel brackets provide anchorage for a ladder to access overhead storage, concealed behind slatted cedar blinds. The floor is medium-density fiberboard, sealed and lacquered; the counter is stainless steel. A glass door allows light in.

FAR RIGHT: A judicious contrast of materials – warm wood and gleaming stainless steel – provides depth of interest in a compact fitted kitchen.

BELOW: Views through to other areas, but particularly external views, prevent small kitchens from feeling too enclosed.

triangle" – sink, stove, and fridge – should be no more than a few paces at most. Small kitchens may rule out certain things, but ease of operation is not one of them.

What small kitchens do rule out is extraneous clutter. Every piece of equipment and every single fixture must earn its keep. Enthusiastic cooks often tend to be kitchenware enthusiasts as well, the sort of people who find it difficult to resist the opportunity to acquire yet another utensil or shiny new gadget. But if you have a small kitchen it's also important to bear in mind that many good cooks accomplish much with the bare minimum and many even swear by the back-to-basics approach. A couple of good saucepans, a frying pan, a casserole, maybe a wok, a few sharp knives, and some basic utensils, such as sieves, a grater, a colander and a few mixing bowls, are really all you need, even to cook the most elaborate meals. Kitchen equipment can be very seductive, but before you give that fish kettle house room, think hard about how often you're really going to use it.

If you have to store cutlery and crockery in the kitchen, you need to keep things simple here, too. Choose oven-to-tableware to avoid the need for separate serving dishes; glasses that you can use for juice, water, or wine; mugs instead of cups and saucers; one set of plain plates that you can use both every day and for special occasions. You'll need less, and what you have will be more uniform in terms of shape and size, which in turn will make it easier to store.

A small kitchen, necessarily, is going to be a single-person operation – there won't be the elbow room for two cooks. It's also going to be a space which is chiefly devoted to cooking. This means you have to be equally ruthless about excluding anything that does not relate directly to this central function. But although a small kitchen is never going to be a living area in the fullest sense, it can be a supremely effective workspace and one that is a pleasure to use.

Saving and enhancing space

Successful small kitchens never feel small – compact, certainly, but not confined. To a large extent, this comes down to tight, rigorous planning that exploits every last inch

of available space. But it also entails adopting various decorative and design strategies to create the illusion of spaciousness.

The most effective small kitchens are generally built-in, for two reasons. A built-in layout allows you to maximize floor area and avoid unnecessary obstacles and protrusions that you have to navigate around. It also has a neater, more seamless appearance, which is equally important. A simple, streamlined approach, with appliances slotted in under a clear line of work surface, and walls devoted to hanging racks of utensils and shelving, provides an inbuilt sense of clarity and order.

It is worth spending considerable time at the planning stage to make sure that you achieve the optimum layout, not merely to make the best use of the available space, but also to insure there is nothing awkward about the arrangement. When you don't have much room to spare in the first place, anything that isn't quite right is bound to become a major source of irritation pretty quickly.

You can pack more into a small kitchen if you opt for slimline or smaller-scale appliances, but you have to be sure that these will adequately serve your needs and also represent a sensible long-term investment (you may move somewhere larger before the appliances have come to the end of their life). Many kitchen manufacturers offer a range of features that allow you to maximize the storage potential of built-in cabinets: pull-out wire baskets so you can use the full height and depth of cupboards, for example, or Magic Corner units that fit into corners and utilize otherwise dead space. Perhaps most useful are pull-out or fold-down preparation areas. Small kitchens tend to be short of counter space, and such features can make the room much more workable on a daily basis.

Decoratively speaking, simplicity is the key: a limited palette of colors and textures avoids visual busyness which can make the room feel even less spacious that it actually is. Light colors and reflective surfaces such as glass and stainless steel, on the other hand, enhance the sense of space. Omitting the plinth at the base of built-in cabinets, so that the feet are exposed and the floor is uninterrupted, can add a sense of visual lightness – just make sure you can clean easily underneath!

Good lighting is essential; recessed or fitted types of lighting, such as downlights, make sense in a small, tightly planned space. You might consider installing internal windows or portholes in partition walls to provide glimpses through to adjacent spaces and borrow additional natural light. If your small kitchen is a self-contained room, it might be worth omitting the door altogether and removing the portion of wall above the door head so the entrance to the kitchen runs all the way from floor to ceiling. It's a relatively minor change, but it can have the effect of making the kitchen seem much less enclosed.

Small kitchens often succeed or fail on the level of detail. Good-looking handles, neat trim and edges, and well-considered junctions between different surfaces can make all the difference.

BELOW LEFT: When space is tight, simplicity of design and fitting is a good strategy, maximizing efficiency and minimizing visual clutter.
BELOW RIGHT: A pull-out table top neatly integrated into a storage wall creates space for eating or working. Pull-out or fold-down features are particularly useful in small kitchen design. **RIGHT:** Pivoting opaque glass doors enclose a small kitchen area within an open-plan space, creating a central box or service core, tucked away from the eating area.

case study: THE SMALL KITCHEN

Small spaces leave next to no tolerance for error. Nicole Morgan's tiny London apartment was originally a studio, with galleried spaces; the redesign, by architect Misha Stefan, arranged it over two levels, three including the roof terrace on top. On the ground-floor level are a bedroom and bathroom, while the open-space living/eating/cooking area is on the first floor where the light is better. Exceptionally tight planning and ingenious spatial strategies now make the whole apartment feel much bigger than it actually is. During the design process, the architect made a cardboard prototype of the basic shapes and tried out a series of different kitchen layouts on Nicole until the fit was absolutely right.

ABOVE RIGHT: Looking from the kitchen through to the adjacent living/dining area. The design challenge was how to fit a practical and workable kitchen within a very narrow, 8ft width. To borrow additional space, the wedge-shaped sink unit is cleverly angled over the stairs. The purple dining table is a classic fold-down design, with the panel fixed on a long piano hinge and supported by a round peg leg. The mosaic tiling around the sink softens the impact of the gleaming stainless steel surfaces.

BELOW RIGHT: The flooring throughout the apartment is light maple, which enhances the sense of space. Walls are white universal plaster sealed with varnish. **FAR RIGHT:** At the far end of the kitchen, a plain plasterboard wall neatly encloses the fridge; behind are the steps up to the roof terrace. The cavity under the stairs has been transformed into a broom cupboard on the left, and houses the boiler on the right, separated from the fridge by an insulated partition.

KITCHEN VERNACULAR

The kitchen's association with food and comfort – indeed with nurturing in general – means that for many people vernacular styles of decoration and design continue to exert a strong appeal. Perhaps the best example of this approach is the ever-popular "country" kitchen, with its scrubbed wooden table, solid fixtures, bunches of drying herbs, and hutch crammed with crockery and homemade preserves. But country kitchens from any country – the kind one might encounter in a simple holiday villa or beach house – share many similar elements and offer many of the same attractions as the more traditional one.

A key characteristic is simplicity. When so much of modern life is dominated by complex technology, technology that most of us don't understand, can't fully operate, and could never begin to fix in the event of breakdown, kitchen vernacular provides a way of regaining control and getting back to a more basic, hands-on way of doing things: Agas rather than microwaves; pantries rather than internet-linked fridges; sharp knives rather than food-processors and so on.

Another element is continuity. Kitchen vernacular is timeless: neither cutting edge, nor rooted in the past. It is an approach that accommodates both old and new, evoking memories of kitchens we might have known as children, while at the same time promising to outlive the latest trends and fads: the type of kitchen you might add to, or subtract from, but never feel the need to redo.

Contemporary country

It's fair to say that the type of country kitchen you see advertised in brochures bears little resemblance to any true country kitchen, past or present. Heavy on the wood, and even heavier on the reproduction detail, such ranges have long promoted a romantic vision of rural life for the benefit of town-dwellers who live miles from the nearest cow. When "country" is so often used as a shorthand for "natural," it's not surprising that people leading stressful urban lives should want to buy into the aesthetic. Such ranges, however, are little more than kitchens in fancy dress. The heart and soul of the vernacular aesthetic is something more elemental, and cannot be produced to a formula.

FAR LEFT: The kitchen forms the heart of this sixteenth-century Tuscan farmhouse. The huge open fireplace is clad in travertine from a nearby quarry; the terrazzo flooring, common in many rustic Italian homes, is a more recent feature. LEFT: Handmade and hand-glazed Moroccan tiles provide a vivid backdrop in this Brussels kitchen. The irregularity and randomness that arise from the craft process give the tiled surface tremendous vitality.

LEFT: A taste for simplicity is a hallmark of vernacular kitchens. Here York stone and metal shelves support African bowls.
BELOW, LEFT TO RIGHT: Traditional Japanese design was the inspiration for this tiny kitchen in a Paris studio. The kitchen is tucked away under a staircase that leads up to a mezzanine; each stair doubles as a drawer or storage space (left). A sliding ricepaper screen separates the kitchen from the bathroom (center). Small appliances are hidden behind medium-density fiberboard doors; a baffle conceals a fluorescent strip lighting the counter. An internal window lets in natural light (right).

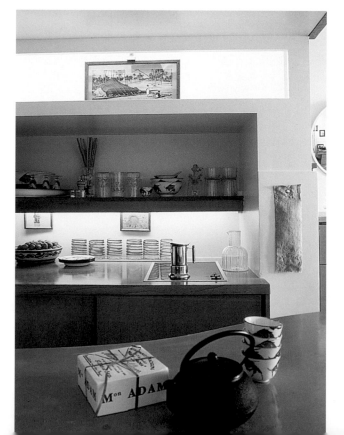

Built-in "country" kitchens often look a little fake simply because traditional kitchens are generally freestanding. Common features of real traditional kitchens include large wooden tables for eating or preparation, hefty butcher blocks, plate rails and racks, hutches, deep apron sinks – all elements that tend to be assembled piece by piece rather than installed as a single package. And no country kitchen worth its salt is complete without an Aga or old-fashioned cooking range. If the kitchen is the heart of the home, the Aga is the heart of the country kitchen: warm, dependable, and decidedly unflashy.

Freestanding cabinets can be compact, but they do work better if there is plenty of room. Better still if you can incorporate the traditional features of the pantry and the scullery. A cool pantry with natural ventilation, lined in slate, marble or other stone, provides the perfect storage conditions for a range of produce, from cooked meats and cheeses to stocks of preserves and wine. A scullery, where dishes can be washed and dried out of general view, can help to make the kitchen itself a more pleasant place for eating and general relaxing.

The country kitchen has always put the focus on natural surfaces and finishes, which are rugged and robust rather than sleek and highly finished. Context is also important here; your kitchen will ring true if you can reflect your surroundings and local area in the choice of materials. Stone, brick, terra-cotta tile, and wood will all age sympathetically and weather well.

Colors, too, come from the same natural palette. Chalky whitewash is an unbeatable background. For a warmer, cozier feeling, natural neutral shades of buff, biscuit and cream, deepening to terra-cotta, complement natural textures very well, while fresher combinations of blue and white have an appealing domesticity and link the modern kitchen with the past.

Country kitchens have long been synonymous with cheerful clutter: hutches chockablock with patterned plates and platters; utensils and pots and pans hanging from racks; fresh produce piled in appetizing displays. There is no doubt that this type of kitchen holds great appeal for those who like to spend hours rummaging through secondhand shops and market stalls for old-fashioned kitchenalia. At the same time, a more contemporary vernacular look can be achieved by shedding some of the visual busyness in favor of a more spare simplicity founded in the elemental contrasts of different surfaces and textures.

Morocco to Mexico

With mass travel to far-flung corners of the globe, our culinary influences are infinitely broader today than they have ever been. Indeed, many people's idea of traditional food is not the traditional food of their own country, but those simple robust dishes and intense flavors they have encountered while far away from home. Increasingly, as evidenced by the exotic produce now regularly stocked by most supermarkets, once people get a taste for Greek, Thai, Tuscan, Moroccan, Mexican, Indian, or Japanese cuisine, they then want to be able to reproduce the full sensory experience in their own kitchens.

A more exotic interpretation of kitchen vernacular draws inspiration from traditional kitchens around the world, such as those one might have come across on vacation. As with the country kitchen aesthetic, these vernacular styles run the risk of looking like "themed" kitchens once transplanted onto home turf: just because you have enjoyed the odd vacation in Tuscany or Tangiers, it doesn't necessarily follow that your kitchen needs to be fully decked out in a simulation of "rustic Italian" or "Moorish" style – what one might term as souvenir. On the other hand, it is perfectly natural to reflect an affection and appreciation for a particular cuisine by adopting elements of that region's traditions in your kitchen decor. Even better if you like to cook in that style: an Eastern-influenced kitchen, for example, makes perfect sense if your favorite utensil is a wok, and five-spice powder regularly features on your shopping list.

Rather than carry out a wholesale makeover, the popular approach adopted by television decorating programs, it's far better to suggest an exotic influence more subtly, relying

FAR LEFT: The elemental quality of basic surfaces and materials is part of the vernacular appeal, as shown in this vaulted kitchen with walls and ceiling made of rubble stone. **LEFT:** A variation on the theme of the traditional country hutch, these glass shelves set over a scrubbed pine table provide plenty of space for a comforting display of kitchen clutter. **BELOW:** Vernacular kitchens tend to include unfitted elements such as the butcher block. **RIGHT:** An easy blend of old and new, this unpretentious kitchen features open shelves and racks of crockery, an old painted table, and a set of 1950s diner chairs.

simply on color and on choice of materials to get the message across. Plain, all-white decorative schemes, luminous, airy and cool, evoke unpretentious hot country living, while more intense colors, such as aquamarine, indigo, orange, and bright yellow, used in luminous washes or glazes have all the *joie de vivre* both of more demonstrative, far-flung cultures and of hotter, spicier dishes. Exuberant tilework and vividly colored ceramics suggest a Spanish influence; ricepaper screens, dark wood, and bamboo reflect Far East culture; while raw plaster walls and terra-cotta tiling call to mind rustic farmhouses of southern Europe.

The underlying appeal of these vernacular traditions, wherever they hail from, lies in the fact that they convey the simple pleasure of food. This directness, of both cooking and serving, serves as an essential antidote to our increasingly pre-packaged lives.

THE PROFESSIONAL KITCHEN

Over the last decade or so, the professional kitchen has become an important point of reference for serious home cooks. With more people choosing to socialize in restaurants and with the increased visibility – indeed fame – of chefs, it's not surprising that the boundaries have become blurred between the domestic and professional spheres. Intense mass media interest in cooking and celebrity cooks has only accelerated the trend. After a particular brand of omelet pan was mentioned in passing on one popular program, the manufacturer of the pan was so swamped with orders that they had to take on extra staff. If we can't always manage to cook with a TV chef's reliability or a restaurateur's flair, it seems we all want to cook with the same "professional" equipment.

For most domestic cooks, the fully fledged professional kitchen is far from a necessity. Even if you pride yourself on your culinary skills and regularly entertain hordes of friends to three-course meals, you are never going to have to produce the sheer quantity and variety of dishes that emerge from the average restaurant kitchen on a nightly basis. Real professional cooking in any halfway ambitious establishment is cooking under extreme pressure in extreme conditions – it's routinely hot, frantic, exhausting, and occasionally dangerous. However daunted you might be at the prospect of cooking for a dinner party, the task pales in comparison with the frenetic activity of a restaurant kitchen in full swing, where dozens of different orders arrive simultaneously, each requiring different ingredients and techniques to execute. Behind-the-scenes accounts of kitchen life, as described by Anthony Bourdain in *Kitchen Confidential* or Andrew Parkinson in *Cutting It Fine*, portray a world of frayed tempers and phenomenal mental and physical effort far removed from the glamorous milieu of the celebrity television chef.

What can you learn from the professionals? Although the professional kitchen does flatter the aspirations of the wannabe cook, there are certain fundamental principles that are relevant whatever your level of skill. To begin with, the professional kitchen is fitted and equipped to take an enormous amount of punishment; if you choose similar surfaces and fixtures, you'll at least be investing in a kitchen with the potential to last a lifetime. Cooks also select their utensils with care – they may not own or use a huge range of knives, for example, but they know which knife will best perform any given task and how to keep it in top condition. But, last, and most important, good professional kitchens are organized for maximum efficiency. In a professional kitchen, wasted effort is wasted time (and money). Applying these principles won't turn you into a starred chef overnight, but you may well find yourself working much more enjoyably and effectively.

Fixtures

Stainless steel is a material that is virtually synonymous with the professional kitchen. No-nonsense, incredibly robust, and with an aura of factory-style precision, stainless steel can be used to clad kitchen surfaces and is often the preferred finish for heavy-duty appliances, fridges, and ranges as well. In the true professional kitchen, stainless steel has obvious advantages: it's hygienic, rustproof, and strong and can take a high degree of wear and tear. At home, such qualities are no less welcome, but advantages must be offset against a relatively high price tag. Maintenance is not entirely trouble-free, either; to preserve the gleaming appearance of stainless steel requires a fair amount of elbow grease and a good proprietary cleaner, such as the type bartenders use to polish their counters to a high shine. If you can't afford stainless steel kitchen cabinetry but like the look, basic wooden cabinets can be dressed up with stainless steel panels.

Glass is another modern material with a professional edge. Toughened glass shelves at upper level, glass-fronted fridges, or glass backsplashes have a crisp modernity in

RIGHT: The sleek professional kitchen, equipped with robust, individual catering-style cabinets and clinical fixtures, has become a reference point for serious cooks.

keeping with the aesthetic. On the floor, pale ceramic tiles, linoleum, or similar materials that are unobtrusive and easy to keep clean strike the right note of efficiency.

Unlike the vernacular kitchen, which is chiefly a modular look, the professional kitchen is fundamentally built-in in style. Streamlined, neatly detailed for minimal visual distraction and easy maintenance, and with cabinet interiors customized with adjustable shelves and pull-out racks, this is the kitchen as a serious working machine. All this puts the emphasis on careful planning to maximize available space and insure that working sequences operate in a logical, seamless flow. In *Kitchen Confidential*, Anthony Bourdain repeatedly praises cooks for their "moves"; a good team of cooks in a busy kitchen does often appear choreographed, displaying an economy of movement and an almost balletic intuition of how to carry through complex and fast-moving sequences without treading on each other's toes. At home, while the need for such finesse is obviously far less acute, tight planning can contribute enormously to the ease of daily and time-efficient kitchen use.

LEFT: A huge ducting vent provides a means of extraction over a long, stainless steel kitchen workbench. The hard-edged aesthetic works particularly well in lofts and other industrial or commercial conversions. **INSET LEFT:** A seductive array of professional kitchen equipment. Every cook can benefit from a decent set of knives and a few robust pans. **ABOVE:** The industrial style of the sleek, sculptural units is tempered by the natural light that pours through two walls of windows. A wheeled unit provides extra storage and preparation space.

One common feature of the professional-style kitchen is the island unit, used as an additional preparation area or as a cooking zone. The island arrangement echoes the typical plan of many restaurant kitchens, where the "piano" or cooking range forms the focus of the working area. Freestanding "work benches" combine sink, cooktop, and counter in one versatile unit.

Although the essential nature of the professional kitchen is built-in, with equipment neatly stowed out of the way behind closed doors, an element of open storage near the working area is a positive asset. Hanging racks for the *batterie de cuisine*, overhead steel or glass shelves for the pots in constant use, and an arrangement of essential condiments and basic ingredients transform cooking into a smooth operation, where reaching for the salt or the sieve is as instinctive as reaching for the gearshift when you're driving a car. There's no prescribed formula. How you arrange matters will depend on the way you cook and what you like to cook.

Professional equipment

At least half the reason why people become enamored of the professional kitchen is the sheer seductiveness of non-domestic kitchen equipment. It's not just the chefs' knives and catering-size pans; increasingly, it's also professional-style toasters, blenders, coffee grinders, juicers...Not so long ago, if you wanted catering style equipment you would have had to visit a supplier specializing in equipment for the trade; nowadays, most kitchen departments stock a full range of professional kitchen products.

Professional cooking ranges have become increasingly popular in recent years. These are serious pieces of equipment, built to withstand considerable battering; many are also seriously expensive. It used to be said that the oven door of a range had to be strong enough to support a man's weight, since standing on the door to clean the ventilation hood was common practice at the end of many kitchen shifts. Needless to say, such robustness is far from essential on the domestic front.

If you yearn for the real thing, but balk at the price tag, an alternative is to source professional fixtures and appliances secondhand. There is nothing down-at-heel or compromised about such a strategy. Because most catering equipment is so robust (and so easy to keep clean) – and because such a huge proportion of new restaurants fail and find themselves forced to close their doors after an embarrassingly short period of time – the trade in second-hand kitchen fixtures is healthy and brisk. You may well pick up a bargain with many serviceable years left to go, for a fraction of what you would pay for the same piece of equipment new.

Professional-quality basic equipment – such as knives and pots and pans – do more than earn their keep. (For a full discussion on the merits of various types, see Fixtures and Appliances, pages 194–197). In this context, it is enough to say that it is certainly worth investing in good basic utensils that have the potential to last a lifetime with proper care and maintenance. Decent, heavy pans that conduct heat properly, generous cast-iron casseroles, and a few knives that can be honed to a razor-sharp edge are professional tools that should be in everyone's kitchen.

Over and above the basics, how you equip your kitchen should relate directly to what you like to cook. No serious chef would put up with a pasta-maker occupying valuable counter space when it was used only half a dozen times a year. If you can't resist impulse buys, at least store your purchases well away from the action.

In many respects, the professional kitchen is a state of mind, a way of organizing yourself so that you work at your most effective. For professional cooks, the "*mise-en-place*" is an arrangement of basic ingredients – such as salt, pepper, oil, and fresh herbs – that they use every shift to create their dishes. Each cook will have a different *mise-en-place* according to what they cook and a different way of arranging it, according to the way they cook and what feels right to them. Setting up and equipping a professional-style kitchen is less about importing status symbols and more about adopting an organized way of thinking.

ABOVE: Acid green walls set off a selection of professional-style kitchen cabinets and catering equipment that was acquired secondhand.

ABOVE RIGHT: Professional equipment is remarkably robust, designed to withstand considerable punishment.

RIGHT: The kitchen as food production line. Robust open shelving and plenty of stainless steel convey a no-nonsense approach to cooking.

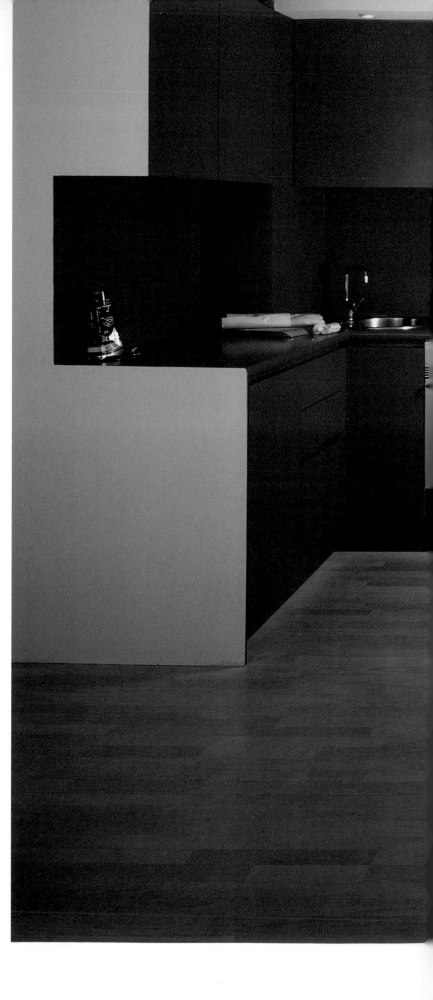

INDOORS AND OUT

Some of the most memorable and pleasurable experiences of eating – and cooking – happen outdoors. Whether it is a family barbecue on a warm summer's evening, a long, leisurely lunch on a vine-shaded terrace overlooking the sea, or a cookout on the beach, food always seems to taste better in the open air. It is small wonder that many people's dream kitchen is one that offers an easy connection between indoor and outdoor spaces.

At least part of the appeal of eating and cooking outdoors is the sense of informality. Outdoor cooking, in particular, is cooking at its most direct and unpretentious – no complicated sauces simmering for hours, simply the basic satisfaction of grilling quickly over high heat and transferring the result straight to the plate. Even better if some of the ingredients and flavors can be picked from your own garden; the smallest urban patch can still support a couple of pots of herbs or a modest crop of tomatoes.

When you are considering how to merge kitchen with garden, it is important to look at the whole issue from both sides so that both indoor and outdoor spaces are conceived as a complementary whole. Sightlines, from vantage points both indoors and out, are important, as is consistency of surfaces and finishes.

Making the connection

Kitchens at ground-floor or semi-basement level obviously offer the greatest potential. But even kitchens located on the upper floors can some provide scope for open-air cooking and eating.

The simplest way to merge indoor with outdoor spaces is to improve the means of access to the outdoors. For ground-floor kitchens this may mean installing French doors in place of a single door, glazing an end wall, enlarging a window, or similar straightforward alterations to bring the outdoors more sharply into view. To enhance the sense of connection, you might consider extending the same type of flooring (or at least the same tone of flooring) from indoors to out: wooden floorboards giving way to a deck,

On upper levels, a balcony
or a roof terrace can provide
enough space to enjoy the
pleasures of outdoor eating
whenever the weather
permits. The inset wall panel,
grouping the light controls, is
a neat detail.

ABOVE: A wrap-around verandah accessible from the kitchen offers a place to enjoy food amid spectacular scenery. **LEFT:** A stone counter running the length of a kitchen and extending into the yard blurs the distinction between indoors and out. **RIGHT:** Windows that lift right up like hatches can instantly transform the kitchen into an airy outdoor room – when the weather allows. The primary cooking area, comprising barbecue and cooktop, is located outside under the deck awning.

FAR RIGHT: The kitchen in this beach house leads directly to a shaded patio. Cabinet doors are made of medium-density fiberboard, which has been lacquered silver and yellow with car paint.

for example, or pale stone or tile repeated on both sides of the boundary between indoors and out. Similarly, it can be particularly effective to extend a counter out into the yard so that it forms a continuous work surface.

Most conventional connections with outdoor areas involve a metal or wooden framework to support glazing or glazed doors. It costs a little more and takes a little more design expertise, but reducing such frameworks to a bare minimum, so that the entire wall dividing kitchen from outdoors effectively reads as an uninterrupted plane of glass, brings the natural world that bit closer.

Extending the kitchen can also provide the opportunity to improve the relationship with outdoor areas. Many row houses in cities have a side passage between the house wall and the neighboring property which is often unusable as outdoor space. Here, it can make sense to redesign the kitchen to absorb this area; toplighting, skylights, or glazed walls will reinforce the connection with the outdoors without any significant loss of outdoor space. Simple glazed additions to kitchens are another very effective way of merging indoors with out. Developments in glass technology mean that glazed expanses no longer need to be problematic. New techniques for jointing avoid the risk of leaks; new types of glass, such as "Low E" (low-emissivity) glass, prevent excessive heat loss in cold weather. If you don't want to remain on full view the entire time, you could opt for photovoltaic glass which allows you to change the glass from transparent to translucent or opaque at the flick of a switch. Panels of colored glass add vibrancy and delight.

Top glazing, roof windows, and skylights are other ways of providing kitchens at upper levels with some sense of connection with the world outside. Depending on the structure of your home, you might also consider creating a roof garden or top-level sunroom adjacent to a kitchen or eating area. At the very least, a balcony that is large enough for a couple of chairs, a table, and a few flowerpots can add a sense of openness to an enclosed kitchen area.

The outdoor kitchen

For those of us who live in temperate regions of the world, cooking outdoors is not a year-round option. But if you enjoy eating and cooking alfresco, it makes sense to set up and equip an outdoor cooking/eating area so you can take advantage of a spell of fine weather whenever it occurs.

Outdoor cooking tends to mean some form of grilling. There is a huge range of barbecues on the market, from basic, hibachi-style disposable trays to massive affairs complete with built-in rotisseries. A popular option, which falls somewhere between such extremes, is the type of drum or lidded bowl barbecue on a wheeled stand which concentrates heat so that food cooks evenly and efficiently all through. Built-in barbecues or grills are not difficult to construct; site them where smoke will not blow indoors but sufficiently close to the kitchen to make preparation and cooking straightforward. If you do opt for a built-in arrangement, you should also provide space around the grill for setting down plates and platters.

If you're cooking outside, chances are you'll want to eat outside as well. An outdoor eating area can be as impromptu as a blanket spread over the grass; tables and chairs, however, turn the yard into a true outdoor room.

Simple, robust outdoor furniture can be surprisingly difficult to track down; the market tends to be dominated by fancy wrought-ironwork in pastiche Victoriana at one extreme and flimsy plastic at the other. Look for canvas director's chairs, plain folding cafe chairs in slatted wood and metal, basic hardwood benches and tables that weather to an attractive patina, or wicker basket chairs for greater comfort. There's no need for outdoor furniture to differ fundamentally in style from furniture indoors: tables and chairs that are light enough to move indoors and out as need and weather dictate are one solution.

Set up an eating area where there is a level surface and where there is an attractive viewpoint and remember to provide shade with an awning, pergola, or trellis. Artificial garden lighting, in the form of flares, candles, lanterns, or strings of lights, adds a magical dimension to evening meals.

As supermarket produce becomes ever more bland and insipid, merging indoors with out provides the chance to grow your own fresh fruit, vegetables, and herbs. In days gone by, the kitchen garden was the essential adjunct to every country house, no matter how modest in size. With food scares constantly hitting the headlines and the growth of interest in organic methods of production, the time is ripe for a revival of these traditional skills. Container-grown herbs could not be simpler or more foolproof; basic salad vegetables such as lettuces and tomatoes demand little expertise. Flavor is fugitive: growing your own cuts the distance between plot and plate to an absolute minimum, maximizing freshness and taste.

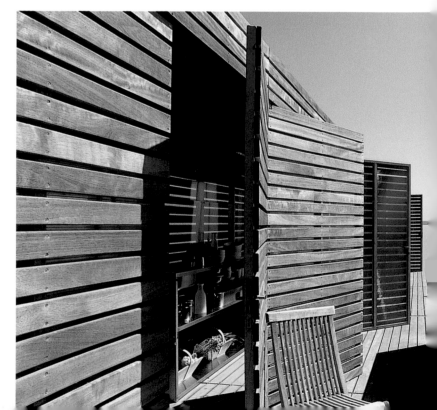

RIGHT: An electronically controlled glass roof slides back to create a sunny open-air eating area. Low-emissivity glass and underfloor heating help to maintain a comfortable indoor temperature on less clement days. **BELOW LEFT:** This outdoor cooking and eating area is simplicity itself, with the slatted structure that houses the preparation area echoing the spacious deck. **BELOW RIGHT:** Food tastes better outdoors, particularly when cooked in a wood-fired oven. **BELOW FAR RIGHT:** An indoor/outdoor kitchen and preparation area cuts the time from pan to plate. The stoves are set into a countertop made of waxed cement.

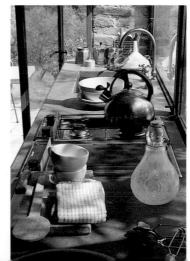

case study: THE INDOOR/OUTDOOR KITCHEN

Running the full width of the house, this large light-filled kitchen merges almost seamlessly with the deck and backyard. When the owners, Winfried Heinze and his partner Heather, bought the property they knew immediately how they wanted it changed. Their previous home had been a tall, narrow row house with limited spatial possibilities. In this house, the greater width made it possible to open out the ground floor completely and fully connect with the outside areas. The kitchen was conceived as the central focus of the house and the intention was to make it big enough that all other activities could happen around it.

ABOVE: The garden is also a productive space – herbs are grown near the house for easy access. **RIGHT:** At the bottom of the garden is a patch where Winfried and Heather grow berries, tomatoes, and salad vegetables. **ABOVE RIGHT:** Looking through the kitchen to the yard. Glazed doors fill the end wall. A floor-level heating channel runs along at the base of the doors so that radiators do not interrupt the space.

Unusually, Winfried and Heather ran the entire scheme themselves, from design to project management, using an architect only to gain the necessary building permits. They sourced many of the materials and fixtures on the internet. The house was stripped back to its bare bones, with most internal walls removed to create a big open space. The glazed end walls, fitted with sliding doors, mean that from any point on the ground floor the entire yard is visible. The airy, spacious quality is a positive advantage for Winfried, a photographer who sometimes works from home.

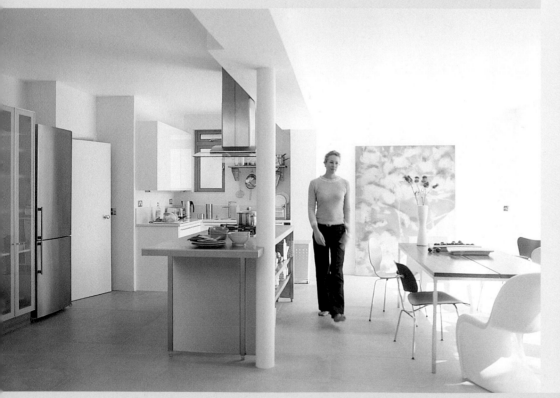

LEFT AND ABOVE: The sleek centerpiece of the kitchen is a stainless steel island, made to the owners' specification by a manufacturer who produces kitchen fixtures for professional applications. The island houses a cooktop and oven; the fridge and ventilation unit were sourced on the internet, which resulted in a considerable saving. **RIGHT:** View from the deck into the kitchen. While work was being carried out, Winfried and Heather rented an apartment nearby, so that daily progress could be closely monitored. The key practical challenge was coordinating the sequence of work.

LEFT: The end wall is filled with four sliding glass doors; the two outer doors slide over the middle pair, leaving a protected zone in the center of the space. This arrangement means that on cooler days people can sit indoors with the doors open without feeling a chill. Indoors the flooring is gray Spanish limestone in large square slabs; outdoors the decking is in ipe, a Brazilian hardwood. The modern dining table, made by a friend, is walnut over an aluminum frame and legs. **RIGHT:** Detail of the stainless steel shelving on one side of the kitchen island. **BELOW:** Built-in cabinets provide storage in the kitchen area, supplemented by tall glass-fronted cupboards for crockery and glassware.

Basic Elements

Work surfaces, flooring, wall treatments, and lighting are the basic elements that will instill a sense of character into your kitchen and, at the same time, help achieve a practical, hardworking room for all your activities. When it comes to making decisions about the choice of surfaces, finishes, and fixtures for your kitchen, it is important to consider both style and efficiency. Will a wooden countertop better suit your needs than a light-up glass version? What type of storage do you prefer? And if you have children, are smudge-prone, stainless steel door fronts really the best option?

These considerations do not mean, however, that practicality should be achieved at the expense of a pleasant and stylish working environment. There can be nothing worse than an unloved, utilitarian kitchen that is bland and dull to be in, and it is possible to combine function with individuality.

Today there is a wealth of materials and fittings adopted for kitchen use. Some hold traditional associations with the kitchen (wood, stone, and ceramic for instance) while others like rubber, glass, and steel have winged their way from the restaurant world or techno industry into our homes. All offer a variety of advantages, and will suit different applications, lifestyles, and budgets.

Such a diverse selection can be both attractive and bewildering at the same time, so the aim of this chapter is to provide you with all the information you need to choose these basic essentials.

ABOVE: Mixing materials is a good way of adding design interest. Dark teak counters and backsplashes are offset by the white sink, maple cabinets, and stainless steel door. **LEFT:** Contrasting floor materials define different zones. The working area features a blue mosaic floor in contrast to the warmer strip flooring in the dining section. An unbroken wall of mosaics throughout unifies the space. **RIGHT:** A raw, sculptural island unit has been fashioned from concrete and appears to rise seamlessly from the concrete tiled flooring. The long wooden table was constructed from two old garden pine trees which fell down during a hurricane.

LEFT: Natural light is crucial for cooking and preparation and helps maintain a connection with the outside world. Here an expanse of clear glass floods the kitchen with an uplifting lightness. **ABOVE RIGHT:** An illuminated backsplash casts an ambient, but practical glow in this alcove. **INSET BELOW:** Sinuous and space age, a sweep of focused spotlights built into the overhead cornice provides very modern task lighting for working by.

LIGHTING

Now that kitchens have become the multifunctional hub of the home – somewhere to cook, eat, and relax – it is important to invest in flexible lighting that can cope with every scenario. Before you choose a lighting system, think about how you use your kitchen. Look at how much natural light the room gets, noting the number of windows, which way they face, and how the light differs according to the time of day and year; then work out how this can be enhanced with artificial lighting. The colors, textures, and materials you choose for countertops, backsplashes, and cabinets will also affect the quality of light. Pale colors reflect light and dark colors absorb it. If your kitchen is made up of richly stained wood cabinets and slate floor tiles, you will need to maximize the light by allocating extra, brighter bulbs. Matte finishes such as sandblasted aluminum diffuse light, while high-gloss surfaces and stainless steel pick up reflections causing glare – this can be minimized by using a frosted lens and adding dimmer switches.

Remember to plan well in advance, as last-minute lighting schemes can limit options and result in disruption and extra cost later. You may want to seek advice from a lighting expert, interior designer, or interior architect, who will have an understanding of the different sources of light, as well as their direction and control. Always employ a qualified electrician to insure a safe and well-fitted installation.

Kitchen lighting divides into two types: task lighting to cook and prepare food by, and ambient lighting for everyday use and for dining and relaxing by.

Task lighting

First and foremost, the kitchen is a hardworking room, so practical needs must be addressed at the outset. Light sources should always be in front of you, rather than behind, to prevent your shadow from coming between you and the task you are working on.

Bright and efficient task lighting is essential for the hardworking element of your kitchen, for preparation, cooking, and washing dishes. Under-cabinet lighting directed over the cooktop, sink, and chopping board will provide focused task lighting. Position lights as close to the front edge of the cabinets as possible, otherwise you will illuminate the back of the counter rather than the activity you are working on. Low-voltage halogen gives a bright, crisp light and bulbs are slim enough to recess into the base of cabinets. Strip lights can also be mounted on the underside of cabinets or shelves and be fitted with baffles or reflectors to subdue glare. For island units, where there are no upper cabinets to affix the light fixture to, choose ceiling-mounted downlights with the right beam width to create focused light. Most extractor hoods now come with built-in lighting to illuminate the cooktop while ovens are usually equipped with interior lights. Light also needs to be reflected directly onto sinks and draining boards. Wherever possible, fit automatic lights to the inside of cabinets so that they will turn on and off as the door opens and shuts.

Ambient lighting

Effective ambient or general lighting will help create different moods. If you have an open-plan kitchen, you will need a versatile scheme with subtle mood lighting as well as bright lights to merge in with the rest of the space. A single dimmable pendant, or row of them, above a table will create an intimate light for eating and help differentiate the dining space from the kitchen's work zones. A rise-and-fall fixture can be pulled down for a cozy candlelit supper or raised for everyday meals and other activities.

The layout and size of your kitchen will dictate the number and arrangement of lights. Take time to position them correctly as lights placed in the center of the room will focus on the floor rather than the perimeter of the room where most of the working kitchen is sited. Track lights and spotlights will wash the walls and surfaces with light while a series of recessed halogens will be less of an obstruction in kitchens with low ceilings. And don't forget that exposed fixtures will collect cooking grime and grease more readily than recessed or semi-recessed lights set flush into a surface. Lights positioned on top of upper cabinets or wall-mounted uplights will visually raise the ceiling and create good general lighting at the same time.

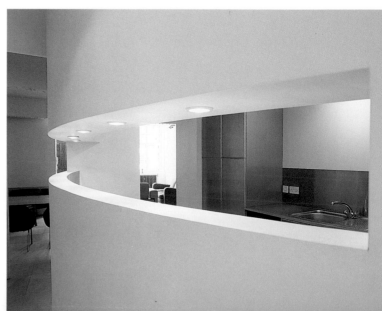

Colored lighting

Many hotels and restaurants are experimenting with colored lighting, not only as a way to alter a room's appearance but also as a way to affect the mood of the people who are in it. The idea is based on the principle that colors stimulate the brain in different ways, for example, indigo for clear thinking and concentration, green for forgiveness and acceptance, and orange for passion and vitality. This type of ambient lighting is more suited to the relaxation zones of the house, but could be used to a limited extent in the kitchen as a dramatic mood-making device. Colored light is not advisable for task lighting.

Types of light

▸ Tungsten or incandescent bulbs are cheap, readily available and easy to use and replace. They come in various styles, colors, and wattages and create a warm, mellow light, which resembles natural light more closely than fluorescent tubes. However, around 90 percent of the energy is converted into heat, not light, so they are not suitable for use near flammable materials. Tungsten bulbs have the shortest lifespan (up to 1,000 hours) so offset the cost by turning the lights down when you aren't preparing food and turn them off when you're not in the kitchen.

▸ Halogen bulbs emit a whiter, crisper light. They are also much smaller, and ideal for adding light unobtrusively, for example, as recessed downlights built into a ceiling. The lamp is filled with halogen gas within which the filament burns. It has a quartz body instead of glass, allowing the halogen lamps to reach much higher temperatures – the light is literally "white hot," so do not install at low level or where hands may come into contact with it. Low-voltage halogen bulbs are even more compact with a lower wattage and are operated via a transformer, as opposed to mains operation. Dichroic halogen lights were developed for the food industry so that the kitchens did not become too hot for the chefs. A special dichroic coating that stops infrared light from passing beyond the bulb means that they radiate a cool beam. Halogen also lasts considerably longer than

FAR LEFT: One-space living requires a variety of lights to accommodate different needs. A row of pendant lights over the dining table creates a more intimate light for eating and sets it apart from the cooking area where directional spotlights are employed. **LEFT:** Recessed downlights make a feature out of this narrow aperture and add extra illumination at the same time. **ABOVE:** Skylights are an effective way of punching natural light into a dark, narrow kitchen but remember to complement with good artificial lighting. Here a large suspended striplight has been installed for evenings and dark mornings.

tungsten (up to 3,000 hours) though the amount of energy used to generate light is more or less the same. Bulbs are fragile and require special handling with a clean cotton cloth as any oil from your fingertips may damage the bulb.

▶ Fluorescent tube lighting is very bright and powerful and should be well baffled and not looked at directly. It used to have a reputation for harsh, flickering light, although this has been improved with newer (and more expensive) dimmable versions. Compact fluorescents are thin tubes that can be folded and enclosed within a pearl bulb for a warmer light. Fluorescents are extremely energy efficient (lasting up to 8,000 hours) with a low-heat emission – an undoubted benefit in a room of heat-generating equipment.

▶ Fiber-optic lighting can create a magical, starry ambience. Light is shone down thin strands of coated fiberglass or acrylic, where it emerges only at the ends. This allows the light source to be placed some distance from the light that is emitted, making it cool at point of delivery. Strands can be touched, bent, or used underwater; in the kitchen fiber-optically lit glass countertops or fiber-optic carpets will add an individual touch. However, it is expensive and comes with a bulky light-source box.

▶ LED (or light-emitting diodes) are the small red lights used in watches and stereos. They are fairly uncommon for the domestic scene, but they are extremely energy efficient (with a 100,000 hour lamp life) and have a very low heat emission. As such, they are ideal for areas that are awkward to replace such as recessed floor uplights.

Light fixtures

Whether you opt for sleek, modern styles or a more traditional, period look, your choice of light fixtures will determine the effect. The common denominator here is that all kitchen lights must suit their assigned task, be easy to clean, and have easily replaceable bulbs or tubes.

▶ Track lighting is most flexible in its "free form" version, where different lights can be fitted at any point along the track and moved along. This allows you to create a lighting system personalized for your needs – for example,

ABOVE: Here, the conventional backsplashes are ingeniously replaced by narrow, sliding windows to allow fresh air and natural light into a confined space. **ABOVE RIGHT:** A row of green glass pendants provides even illumination over the work surface when natural light fails.

BELOW RIGHT: Natural light has been enhanced as much as possible in this top-floor kitchen by the installation of large windows and a ceiling made of flat panes of glass. In addition to this, a section of glass bricks in the floor allows light to filter in from downstairs.

spotlights at the working end of the kitchen and a pendant in the dining area. The more reasonably priced "fixed" track usually has around four permanent light fixtures, which cannot be repositioned. Track can be mounted vertically or horizontally, on the wall and ceiling. However, it can be intrusive and also reminiscent of a shop's display lighting and is only suitable for modern kitchens.

▸ Downlights can be recessed or semi-recessed into the ceiling or under cabinets to provide effective task lighting. They are dimmable and come in different beam widths. Directional downlights are even more flexible.

▸ Spotlights use incandescent reflector bulbs that are silvered on the inside, or low-voltage halogen. They can be fitted onto a track system or directly onto a surface.

▸ Wall lights and wall washers create a subtle form of background light. They are good for creating mood lighting for areas meant for eating and relaxing.

Control systems

Dimmer switches are an excellent way of creating a soft, ambient glow for dining in the kitchen. They reduce the amount of light by decreasing power to the light source, extending the life of the lamp at the same time. Dimmers are available in rotary/push button, touch-control, and remote-control versions. For the ultimate scene-setting device, intelligent light systems allow you to create and then recall pre-set light patterns at the touch of the button. You can also pre-set lighting to switch on or off at certain times and to respond to changes in natural light levels.

Switches

Stick to simple, unfussy switches in wipe-clean materials such as plastic, brushed nickel, Plexiglas, and chrome. Install them at elbow height, so that even if your hands are full, they can be flicked on or off with relative ease. If the kitchen is large and has more than one entrance, each lighting area should have its own switch so it can be controlled separately. This offers maximum flexibility and economy, allowing you to illuminate one half of the kitchen at a time.

WALLS

As with any room, kitchen walls come alive with color and texture. A kitchen with plain-fronted, blonde wood cabinets may benefit from a solid block of bright color or a band of shiny glass mosaic. On the other hand, kitchen cabinets that make a statement of their own, either with a strong color or with an unusual wood grain, will probably suit a more neutral backdrop.

Color and decoration aside, kitchen walls need to be practical and hardwearing. No other room in the house is bombarded with the same combination of wet and dry heat, dust, fats, and oils. Smooth finishes are far better in a busy kitchen – a textured surface with too many undulations will be harder to wipe clean.

Material choices

Paint This is a brilliantly simple way to add color to kitchen walls and surfaces. Latex chalkboard paint can be used to create a smooth, hardwearing writing surface. Choosing a color scheme from a color card is difficult, so it is always wise to buy sample pots first for accuracy and also to look at the color at different times of the day.

The hot, humid conditions of a kitchen call for a durable paint finish. Oil-based eggshell is a good choice, as it creates a semi-sheen finish that can be wiped down easily. Latex velvet is another. A tough and washable water-based paint with a hardwearing and scuff-resistant silky finish, it can be bought with various sheens, from shiny to satin to an almost matte look and feel. Flat latex is less durable and is better

LEFT: Bare plaster painted a rich, deep shade of brown adds a rugged, natural touch. Colorful kitchen paraphernalia hung on a simple chain provide all the color that is needed. **RIGHT:** Metro-style white tiles are clean and hardwearing and completely at home in this modern country kitchen. **BELOW RIGHT:** Exposing the original brickwork on one wall retains a sense of character in this warehouse conversion, while stainless steel counters bring the look completely up to date.

suited to kitchen ceilings. Many stores now sell paints specifically designed for the damp, moist conditions of kitchens. They have a soft sheen finish that is moisture-resistant, tough and durable, and easy to wipe.

Good preparation will add years to your paintwork. Use degreaser soap and water to wash down all surfaces, starting with the ceiling, and allow to dry before painting. If there are any damp patches, find the cause and remedy it. When dry, coat with a primer/sealer. Plaster surfaces with nicotine stains also need to be coated with primer/sealer. Older houses may have a coating of calcimine. Wash and scrape off as much as possible and cover with stabilizing solution before repainting. Any cracks and holes should be filled and then lightly sanded, prior to the main coat.

Plaster Bare plaster is a very durable and inexpensive finish. If you plan to paint the surface, the plaster needs to be primed first with a diluted coat of latex. You can create depth and character on plaster by working in powdered paint for a marbled effect. Or instead, several coats of tinted limewash will build up a soft, chalky bloom of color, while the addition of metallic dust will create a sparkling surface. A water-based waxy glaze will add subtle shading, but remember to seal it with a coat of flat varnish for a hardwearing surface.

ABOVE LEFT: Glass bricks allow light to filter in subtly from an adjoining room, creating a softer division than a solid wall would, and intensifying the color of the bright cabinets and ergonomic curves. **TOP:** Simple tongue-and-groove paneling in a muted olive green creates a distinct Shaker feel – a warm and welcoming setting where the natural hues of herbs and spices are the best form of decoration. The uniformly spaced jars provide a visual contrast to the vertical lines of the paneling. **ABOVE:** A wall of bold paintwork enlivens the blocky, freestanding steel units and task lamps.

Tiles Hardwearing and water-resistant, ceramic tiles are ideal for kitchen walls. They are made from clay fired at very high temperatures to strengthen them, and they come in a wide choice of size, color, and design. Hand-painted decorative tiles and colorwashed crackleglaze tiles look effective in older houses while steel-effect tiles with stud and grille textures will add an industrial edge to any kitchen. Specialist companies can create one-off designs and colors to order; or search for antique tiles at flea markets or salvage yards. You can also commission ceramic tiles digitally printed with your own design or image. Vitrified tiles have a low water absorption (between 0.5 and 3 percent) and are more dense and durable than earthenware tiles. Most floor tiles are vitrified although glazed vitrified wall and cladding tiles are becoming increasingly popular.

Wall tiles are subject to less wear than floors, so are thinner; they are also easier to work with and cut or snap to a scored line. Glass mosaic tiles or smooth, matte tiles can create a sleek and practical backsplash. Remember that all unglazed tiles must be sealed.

Tiles can be stuck to most walls as long as the surface is flat, clean, dry, and stable. Old wallpaper must be removed, and gloss-painted walls must be sanded down to provide a key for the adhesive. You can tile on top of old ceramic tiles providing they are clean and degreased but stagger the edges away from the old ones for extra strength. Old tiles can be refreshed by simply painting over them. Use a tile primer as a basecoat and then brush with a tile gloss for a mirror finish and a brand-new look.

Wallpaper Don't overlook wallpaper. Seek out good-quality vinyl wallpapers, which are moisture-resistant and steam-proof. Wallpaper designs have come on hugely in recent years, and are now available in a range of sophisticated patterns and modern designs including metal effects, glossy lacquers, even faux snakeskin. As an alternative to covering the entire room, one or two panels can be used as an accent or printed with a photo mural or image. Tough, textured paper provides a way to disguise uneven walls.

Wood A popular material for the kitchen, wood is most commonly used on counters, flooring, and cabinet doors. Not only is it a warm, attractive, and natural material, it is easy to keep clean with a damp cloth and mild detergent. Wood falls into two categories. Hardwoods come from broad-leaved, deciduous trees which shed their leaves in the winter months, such as oak, ash, beech, and maple. Softwood is a timber from any coniferous, evergreen tree, for example, pine and spruce, and can be used for covering walls or ceilings in tongue-and-groove boards.

There are many species to choose from. Oak has a rich tone and classic grain; beech is a popular wood in a pale, light tan color. Beech and oak can also be stained to achieve the rich, tawny look of a tropical timber. Cherry is one of the best woods for the kitchen and will deepen over time into a bronze shade; maple is a straight-grained light wood; and iroko is a solid wood from Africa, similar to teak. It is naturally oily and deepens to a rich brown.

Character oak which displays the wood's natural features such as knots, clusters, and splits exudes a quintessential English look that is perfect for country kitchens, while pickled, frosted, and bleached oak yields a much lighter, more contemporary finish. Ash, beech, sycamore, and maple are blonder woods, and will provide a more neutral backdrop. Tropical woods such as teak, iroko, and wenge should always be bought from reclamation or salvage yards. Rare or environmentally protected species should only be bought if they are from sustainably managed forests and new wood from well-managed woodlands. Check with your dealer; although most manufacturers use sustainable forests, it can take over 100 years for an oak tree to reach maturity.

Tongue-and-groove paneling is one of the easiest ways to liven up a kitchen and conceal uneven and crumbling walls. Painted in a cool white or a muted blue or clear varnished, it will bring a distinct Shaker style to the room. Seal wooden wall surfaces against damp and stains, and insulate with metal sheets or fireproof material if they are adjacent to the stove.

case study:
THE MATERIALS KITCHEN

Using contrasting materials and finishes on surfaces is a tried and tested way of adding depth of character to a room, but even within the same broad family there can be distinctive variations of tone and texture. In this Manhattan loft kitchen, designed by architect, Moneo Brock, the interplay of different types of wood creates a warm and lively effect. The utilitarian character of the space, expressed in the massive exposed oak beams and pillars, is tempered by smooth painted plaster surfaces and sleek flooring.

LEFT: Douglas fir strip flooring, laid on the diagonal, adds a dynamic quality to the space. The dining table is made of yellow pine; kitchen cabinets are faced in pale birch. The facing panels on the box-like divider enclosing the kitchen area are oriented strandboard, a type of cheap manufactured board more commonly used as temporary boarding for shop fronts. RIGHT: A strandboard-faced divider partitions the kitchen area from the main loft space. The more somber grooved draining board and countertops are made of slate.

COUNTERTOPS AND BACKSPLASHES

Countertops are probably the hardest-working element of your kitchen, subjected to a daily onslaught of knocks, spills, hot pans, sharp knives, and the occasional human being (for who hasn't clambered onto a counter to change a light bulb or reach the back of cupboards?). Strength and resilience are the greatest priority, but countertops must also be hygienic and easy to wipe clean. The best ones resist the abrasive effects of scouring and will not absorb the stains from food, vinegar, and oil. If possible use one length of countertop, keeping seams to a minimum. This way there will be less opportunity for bacteria and dirt to build up in crevices. For similar reasons, sinks should be either flush-fitted or undermounted into the counter. Select the thickest countertop you can afford. The most common thicknesses are 1¼in and 1½in, but a 1½in countertop tends to have greater resistance to heat and damage and is less prone to cracking or warping.

The material you choose will mainly depend on personal preference, style of kitchen, and budget, but keen cooks may wish to use more than one countertop material in the same kitchen, specific to an intended activity. For example, an area of smooth, cold marble is ideal for rolling pastry, end-grain maple makes the perfect chopping board, while a section of stainless steel around the cooking area will double as a sleek pan rest. Don't overcomplicate the room with too many materials, however, especially in a small kitchen; as an alternative, use loose cutting boards, which can be moved from area to area and washed easily.

The backsplash is the wall area between the upper and lower cabinets, and as its name suggests is subjected to a daily onslaught of water, grease, steam, liquids, and rogue cooking ingredients. As such, it must be water-resistant and easy to clean. Use a heat-resistant surface such as stainless steel, tile, or stone around the stove, and don't overlook the seam between the counter and the backsplash, which is a potential dirt trap and breeding ground. Fill it with a special rubber sealant; or if you opt for wood, invest in a matching upstand which is attached between the back edge of the countertop and the wall. Even better, use a continuous sheet of material to create a one-piece, seam-free countertop and backsplash.

Material choices

Wood Looks aside, wood is also extremely hygienic, and possesses a natural acidity that inhibits bacterial growth (see page 129 for more general information). This makes it a great surface for food preparation, but it is important to treat the wood so the countertop can withstand the heat, moisture, and heavy use of a working kitchen. Oiled solid hardwood, such as teak, oak, or iroko, is probably the best option, as it is most resistant to heat and stains and tends to improve with age. The silky, oiled finish also enhances the color and grain of the wood and creates a surface that is easy to clean. The countertop will usually come pre-oiled; however, after installation, it should be sanded lightly and given an extra layer of oil for further protection. After the initial treatment, only simple maintenance is required with the occasional re-oiling. Any scratches or discoloration can be removed with fine sandpaper, then the surface should be re-oiled and left to dry. A lacquered wood is not so hardwearing, and hot and cold fluids will eventually break down the lacquer so it should be reapplied annually. However, it is more reasonably priced. End-grain wood turned on its end and glued together in blocks or slats gives a very dense surface, ideal for butcher blocks – maple is a good choice as it won't flavor foods.

If a washing machine or dishwasher is to be installed under a wooden countertop, a moisture barrier is required, which is glued to the underside. You must allow a ventilation gap of at least 1in around appliances and between the ends of freestanding stoves (a minimum of 1½in if you have a range). Remember that solid wood works across the grain, so it must be installed to allow expansion and contraction.

RIGHT: Thick slabs of Carrara marble add a further purist's touch to this sleek, uncluttered kitchen, in stark contrast to the abundance of natural foliage outside.

Glass Sheets of toughened ¾in or 1in glass are extremely resilient, hygienic, and easy to clean, and create attractive, modern countertops. The glass is available as transparent, milky, or totally opaque in a myriad of colors, including metallic and pearlescent finishes. It can be color-enameled on the underside and even illuminated with fiber-optic lighting, but this can be extremely expensive. Glass does naturally scratch, although glass with a textured underside will "refract" any scratches on the smooth surface. A finely textured "orange peel" top layer will disguise any scratches. Toughened glass will shatter safely into millions of tiny pieces, but this type of safety glass cannot withstand large cutouts for a sink and cooktop. Non-toughened glass may be a better option and it is still safe, as it has a film applied to the back to hold the shards of glass in place should the counter shatter. Practically, it is far more flexible, allowing for cutouts and special edge finishes. Even though non-toughened glass can take temperatures of up to 104°F, it is still advisable to use a piece of toughened, heat-resistant glass around the cooktop area as it may crack if a hot pan is placed on it. Glass is a good option for backsplashes and can be fixed simply with bolts or silicone glue. Much thinner sheets of glass are used, around ⅜in to ½in, and can also be back-lit to create a mesmerizing glow. Colored or opaque glass is a good choice if you want to hide uneven plaster or unsightly marks on the wall or you could paint the underside with special glass paint.

Stainless steel An increasingly popular choice for countertops and backsplashes, stainless steel will add a professional edge to your kitchen. Good-quality steel is also hardwearing, hygienic, and heatproof and should be at least ⅜in (0.9mm) thick with an 18/8 grading. If it is any thinner, the counter may flex under pressure.

Stainless steel is available in brushed, polished, and patterned finishes. Counters can be fitted with an integral sink, draining board, and backsplash for a streamlined, seamless finish to minimize the number of joints.

Smudges and fingerprints are inevitable by-products of usage, but maintenance is simple – wash with water and a mild detergent and polish dry with a soft cloth. A thin coating of baby oil applied with a dry cloth will bring a sheen back to a smeared surface. Stainless steel is also susceptible to scratches, although over time these will meld together into a patina that will reflect the use they have been put to.

Zinc With a grayer, duller, more seductive sheen than stainless steel, zinc is gaining popularity for counters. Thin sheets of roofing zinc can be glued to a base of medium-density fiberboard and wrapped around and attached to the front edge. Any joints should be soldered. Zinc does scratch

and stain, but this adds to its charm; eventually the counter will develop a soft, burnished patina. Zinc is heat- and water-resistant and easier to clean than stainless steel (fingerprints aren't as obvious) – it also comes with a cheaper price tag.

Stone Natural stone is an excellent material for counters, hardwearing and robust with a cool surface ideal for food preparation. There are myriad different colors and textures available and most come in a polished or matte finish. All surfaces except polished granite should be sealed (most are supplied pre-sealed from the factory) and a wipe with a damp cloth is all the maintenance required. Avoid scouring powders and cream cleaners as they can contain abrasives that may dull the surface.

FAR LEFT: Characterful and well-used, this solid old dresser has a worn wooden top for preparing food. The rustic ambience is complemented by a stainless steel range. **LEFT:** This impressive island unit tempers the sterility of the all-white cabinets along the wall and vast extractor fan by incorporating a smooth block of pale, silvery wood and turquoise cabinets. **ABOVE LEFT:** An uninterrupted line of stainless steel creates a hygienic and hardwearing work surface. **ABOVE RIGHT:** Milky-green glass backsplashes create subtle color against a stainless steel surface.

For a stone backsplash you will only need a veneer thickness as it does not have to withstand any heavy weight or pressure. Countertops need to be much thicker to create a robust and solid preparation surface, but you should remember that a length of solid stone can be extremely heavy as well as expensive and will require sturdy cabinets underneath.

GRANITE This is a high-density stone which is extremely hardwearing and almost impossible to scratch or chip. It is also heatproof (hot pans can be placed directly on the surface), waterproof, and difficult to stain, making it a brilliant choice for kitchen counters. In addition to these attributes, the cool, smooth surface is ideal for food preparation.

Granite is available in a wide range of colors, often with bold natural markings and rich, deep tones, including green, black, and earthy brown. Countertops are cut to size and can be honed to a smooth, matte, eggshell finish. Granite is a crystalline material which is more susceptible to cracking if not adequately supported. If possible, use it in a greater thickness or fix it to a medium-density fiberboard sub-base.

MARBLE These counters provide a cold, hard surface, ideal for pastry making. However, they can be easily stained by acids such as sugar, alcohol, and lemon juice. Some marbles are more dense and less porous than others; always specify a honed finish. Or use an inset slab of marble for kneading and combine it with a different material elsewhere.

LIMESTONE This stone tends to come in light, natural tones like honey, buff, and pale cream, although rich blue/gray varieties are available. It has subtle textures and natural veining with a smooth, matte finish for even wear and tear. Most limestone is porous and should be protected with multiple layers of sealant to prevent staining and acid erosion. Again, limestone is not really recommended for full countertop use in a hardworking kitchen.

SLATE Less expensive than other stones, slate counters can create a dramatic look in your kitchen. With a honed, velvety-smooth finish, slate is available in black and deep tones of blue, green, and silvery gray. It is hardwearing and resistant to heat, and it wipes clean with a damp cloth. Make sure you choose a slate with a high silica content and add a protective sealant to reduce the porosity. More porous slates will absorb oils and stain easily. Surface scratches can be removed with gentle sandpapering.

Pyrolave This material is made from volcanic lava stone that has been fired in the earth's own kiln, which means it can withstand the hottest temperatures that a busy domestic kitchen can inflict on it. Pyrolave has a delicately crazed surface and resembles one large slab of ceramic tile, but without the grout. Design, color, and texture can be applied to the surface.

Solid surfaces These are also known as composite materials and should not be confused with solid, natural stone. Instead, composites are a man-made, non-porous material, made up of acrylic resins and natural minerals – hence the name "composite." The result is an extremely practical countertop that is stain-resistant, waterproof, and very durable. It has a smooth, silky surface that is warm to the touch. The color runs throughout the thickness of the material, making it renewable – any scratches, burns, or dents can be gently sanded down and polished to create a new, blemish-free surface.

Composites like Corian and Paracor can be cut, carved, routed, and sandblasted into any curve, twist, or shape, making it a highly desirable choice for complicated design ideas. Sheets of solid surface can be joined without any seams, creating a sleek countertop, eliminating dirt and

ABOVE LEFT: A bright laminate counter and seamless backsplash are not only practical and robust, but also enliven a functional area.
ABOVE RIGHT: Gray stone countertops with an integral, grooved draining board temper the deep eggplant of the cabinet doors. RIGHT: The burnished gleam of zinc has been wrapped around countertops and side panels, creating an unusual contrast with the white door fronts. The tangerine cupboard is designed as a solid block of color and some of the doors fold down to double as a desk or counter.

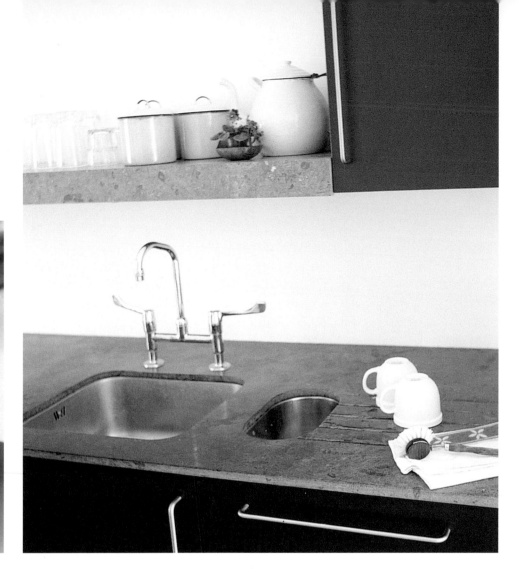

bacteria traps. It can also be combined with an inset solid-surface sink (in the same or a contrasting color) or a grooved integral draining board, or inlaid with steel rods for a built-in pot rest.

The range of color and pattern available is diverse, from a cool glacier white to a speckled granite effect to bold blocks of a single color in hot orange and yellow. All solid-surface counters are made to order and must be installed by a professional fabricator which will increase the already high overall price.

Laminates Forget the peeling, dreary, and faded laminate counters that are so reminiscent of the 1970s. These days, laminates are high-quality products and come in an exhaustive palette of colors and finishes, such as plain matte tones, convincing woodgrains, and subtle patterns to match any style of kitchen. They are extremely reasonably priced and hardwearing, with an easy-to-maintain surface that can also withstand high temperatures and a certain amount of knocks and scratches.

A high-pressure laminate is made up of many layers of colored or patterned paper impregnated with resins. These are fused under high pressure and heat and covered with a clear melamine overlay – the whole structure is then glued to a particleboard, plywood, or medium-density fiberboard substrate. Look for a moisture-resistant backing on the underside that will provide extra protection.

Harsh and abrasive cleaners can scratch and dull the finish, while prolonged wetting or flooding may warp the surface of the laminate. Once damaged, laminates usually cannot be easily repaired. Any seams and marks are fairly hard to disguise, and you end up having to replace the surface entirely.

Solid-core laminates are a more hardwearing option, with solid color running throughout the thickness of the material. They can be used to make thinner countertops than the standard thickness – ¾in as opposed to 1½in – and give a sleeker look. Laminate countertops can be made with a curved edge to get rid of sharp corners.

Tiles Despite their strength and water-resistance, tiles are best used for backsplashes rather than countertops, although vitrified tiles can work well (see page 129 for more information). The tile itself is simple enough to clean but the grout in between is easily stained with foods, liquid, and dirt. Unless you use an epoxy grout or are prepared to re-grout regularly, ceramic tiles are better for creating a striking backsplash than for a countertop. They come in a huge choice of size, color, and design, including plain, glossy, matte, metallic, and patterned, or try rows of tiny mosaics in glass, ceramic, or stone. For ease of use, buy sheets of mosaics mounted on a mesh backing. Instead of sticking each mosaic individually, the sheets can be cut to size and stuck directly on the wall.

Concrete These countertops add an earthy, textural element to a kitchen. Unlike the concrete used in pavements, a concrete countertop is mixed with additives to make it less susceptible to chipping and cracking. Counters are usually cast in situ, at your home and on top of existing kitchen carcases. The top is then ground to a polished surface and treated with a special sealant, making it impervious to oil, food, and water, yet retaining a natural look.

Anti-bacterial products You may want to think twice before you buy one of the many "anti-bacterial" products that have been launched for domestic kitchen use. The performance of such anti-bacterial detergents and impregnated chopping boards, dish cloths, and bin liners – even sinks and counters – varies widely in terms of killing bacteria, decontaminating surfaces, or inhibiting bacterial growth. They may even do more harm than good according to some infection experts. Anti-bacterial products share a common characteristic with antibiotics in that they have the ability to kill all bacteria, both good and bad. The most sensitive germs are initially destroyed, leaving behind the germs with some natural resistance, strains that have been termed "superbugs" by some members of the medical world. With the beneficial bacteria gone, these "superbugs" reproduce into bacteria that are virtually impervious to traditional treatment. Experts recommend using good old-fashioned bleach in the kitchen rather than newer anti-bacterial products. Other advice includes getting rid of dishpans, which can encourage cross-contamination of germs between chopping boards, plates, and knives, and using disposable paper cloths instead of tea towels, which could spread infection. Remember, we need good bacteria to fight the bad ones.

BELOW LEFT: Honed concrete counters are a natural foil for the mixture of petrol blue doors and dulled metal panels. A line of cooking oils and pots and pans adds color to these bare surfaces. **BELOW CENTER:** Hardwearing materials that transcend passing trends are often the most successful, like this uniform grid of white mosaic tiles – clean, efficient, and timeless. **BELOW RIGHT:** Dark gray slate tiles form the backdrop for wall-hung brass faucets and simple white pots crammed with utensils. The effect is simple, subtle, and honest.

RIGHT: Long lengths of solid timber planks create a fluid and unified floor. Wood should always be sealed to protect it from moisture. **BELOW LEFT:** Blue natural stone sourced from Belgium completes the natural palette of materials in this galley kitchen. **BELOW CENTER:** Italian travertine floor tiles with a smooth, honed finish are both tough and slip-resistant. The surfaces can contain natural open pores that are normally filled with grout on installation or are pre-filled at source. **BELOW RIGHT:** Painted white floorboards disguise any mismatched woods, blemishes and discrepancies as well as maintaining the freshness of this all-white decor.

FLOORING

A kitchen floor is primarily about comfort, durability, and maintenance. Color and design are, of course, important factors, but the type of surface material you choose needs to fulfill far more demanding practical requirements. A stone floor will last for generations and acquire the lovely patina of use and age, but it is much colder and noisier than vinyl or linoleum, and is an unforgiving surface if you are on your feet all day long. Stone and tiled floors create crisp, functional surfaces but are hard on glass or china – breakages are more likely to occur, perhaps more frequently if you have small children. If you have an open-plan kitchen, you may want to define different zones by using contrasting floor materials or different floor heights. If the kitchen is a small area, however, you should use the same material to convey fluidity and unity.

Whichever type of flooring you choose, it is always better to get it laid by a professional who can advise on substrate, quantity required, and any special finishes or treatments that will extend the life of the floor.

Material choices

Wood A timber floor is simple, versatile, and naturally beautiful. There are many species to choose from, including creamy, variegated maple; reddish brown cherry; oak; and rich dark brown, almost purple-black, walnut. Softwoods such as pine are less expensive and a good choice if you are going to stain or paint the floors. (See page 129 for more information.) For a more decorative look, choose parquet flooring laid in blocks and panels.

Wood is a natural, living material so variations in batches and packs are a matter of course. Wood floors are also very sensitive to their surrounding climate, expanding in damp, humid conditions and shrinking when the air becomes dry. The boards therefore need to be acclimatized before they are fitted, at least 48 hours prior to installation. As such, seasonal cracking – small cracks between boards – is a common occurrence and should therefore be viewed as a characteristic of wood floors.

Wood floors should also be sealed to protect them from the damaging effects of water. Natural boards may come pre-sealed with a wax, oil, or lacquer, but painted or stained floors should also be sealed.

A veneer of hardwood may be a good choice if you want the look of solid wood but haven't got the height space for joists. It is also less expensive than solid wood. A wood laminate floor is cheaper again.

Dirt and grit will act like sandpaper and destroy the protective surface of a wood floor, so vacuum, sweep, and mop regularly. Area rugs or mats can be used to protect high-traffic walkways and standing zones, such as in front of the sink and the fridge. Timbertec treatment leaves a wood floor neutral without varnish.

Tiles and brick Glazed tiles and mosaics do not require any sealing or finishing, whereas unglazed versions need to be oiled and sealed when they are laid or they will absorb water and stain easily. The finish will need redoing periodically to keep the floor in good condition. Encaustic tiles differ from ordinary tiles in that the pattern actually runs through the tile. The stoneware or clay is still in a semi-liquid state while the design is formed and produces the characteristic merging of colors.

Floor tiles are thicker than wall tiles so they will be harder to cut. Bear in mind also that tiling raises the floor level, so you will need to plane down the bottom of doors for extra clearance.

Porcelain tiles are denser and stronger than clay and available in larger slabs. They have a crisp, square edge that can be butted up tightly with minimum grout to produce an almost seamless floor.

Terra-cotta tiles are also made from clay which is baked or fired. Terra-cotta retains heat and is therefore the warmest tile underfoot. Colors range from rich, dark earthy terra-cotta to lighter shades of honey and ocher. Reclaimed and antique terra-cotta tiles have a leathery patina; they are usually molded by hand, and some are even stamped with the maker's original monogram. Terra-cotta should be sealed

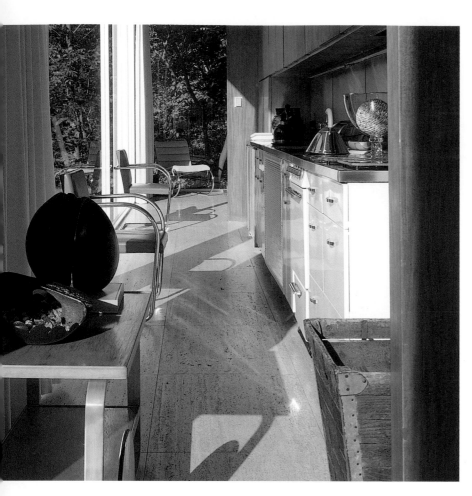

before and after grouting and finished with a paste wax. Regular waxing enhances the natural color and provides protection against staining.

Flooring bricks are non-slip and waterproof. They can be laid in a variety of patterns on damp-proofed concrete. Highly fired, they need no finish but are difficult to clean.

Mosaic Built up from tiny tesserae of stone and marble, mosaics are used to create infinite designs, patterns, and motifs. Special commissions are costly, however; instead, use sheets of flooring mosaics mounted on mesh for easy fixing and add simple borders to define edges. Mosaics need to be grouted if they are to have a finished appearance and cared for like tiles.

Stone Stone floors are solid, tactile, and enduring. Choose from limestone, slate, granite, sandstone, marble, and travertine (a limestone/marble mix) depending on the color and finish you want to achieve (see pages 135–136 for more details). A honed, matte finish will create an anti-slip surface while a riven stone like slate may have surface flaking.

Floor bases need to be clean, dry, and free of grease and loose debris. If the subfloor is not concrete, consult a qualified structural surveyor to make sure it can take the weight of the stone. Screeded or previously tiled floors are easiest to tile onto. Wooden floors require marine ply to be glued and screwed at 6in intervals. All stone should be sealed, waxed, or impregnated (depending on the type of stone) to prevent staining and acid erosion.

ABOVE LEFT: Farnsworth House by Mies van der Rohe. The rectilinear structure, divided by flat planes or service blocks, and widespread use of glass are complemented by travertine and marble. ABOVE RIGHT: Polished concrete floors add a sophisticated earthiness to this kitchen. RIGHT: The irregular surface veining of these green marble floor tiles gives an almost sea-like, watery effect to this Austrian kitchen. The inherent pattern is in stark contrast to the uniform lines of the cement countertop and graphic shapes of the appliances and furniture.

Concrete A utilitarian substance made up of cement powder, sand, and water, concrete floors are affordable and inject a cool austerity into the kitchen. Slabs or tiles must be sealed against stains, and can be waxed or stained to give a more lustrous finish. Concrete can chip and crack.

Terrazzo A mix of glass or marble chippings and resin, terrazzo is hand-troweled onto the floor and ground to a smooth, polished surface. It is smooth, tough, non-slip, and available in any color. Terrazzo must be laid on a stable, non-moving surface such as concrete – an unstable surface may be prone to cracks. A hand-troweled resin is preferable to a roller finish, which is much thinner and therefore prone to cracking. Terrazzo washes clean with hot, soapy water.

Linoleum Once regarded as dreary and old-fashioned, linoleum has now become fashionable. It is extremely durable, flexible, hygienic, and easy to clean, as well as being warm and quiet underfoot. It is made in an environmentally responsible way from natural raw materials such as linseed oil, resin, wood-flour, and chalk. The material is rolled into sheets and pressed onto a burlap backing (or polyester for the tile format) then baked at high temperatures. Linoleum is resistant to acids, oils, fats, and grease although spillages should be removed quickly. Marks left as a result of stubbing out cigarettes can easily be removed with fine sandpaper. Linoleum comes with a factory finish to aid maintenance; spills, mud, and dust can be quickly and easily wiped away. Colors range from neutral shades such as ivory and charcoal to vibrant hues like apple green and indigo, in plain and marbled finishes. Borders, square insets, and feature panels can be added for a more dramatic look. Precision-cutting technology means you can also create unique designs.

Vinyl This flooring is functional, comfortable, and low-cost. High-quality vinyl is thick and made from 100 percent polyvinyl chloride (PVC), hence the name "vinyl." Cheaper versions contain fillers that make them more brittle. Vinyl is ideal for kitchens, is available in an almost unrivaled range of colors, patterns, textures, and designs, and can simulate virtually any type of hard flooring such as wood, stone, or tiles. A hardwearing vinyl is waterproof, slip-resistant, odor- and mildew-resistant, and simple to keep clean (with regular sweeping, and mopping with a mild detergent). The subfloor needs to be clean, level, smooth, and dry before the vinyl is laid. Another benefit is that vinyl is not thick like most natural flooring so there is no need to plane the bottoms of doors and baseboards when it is installed.

Rubber A favorite with architects and interior designers, rubber is practical, hardwearing, warm, water-resistant, burn-resistant, and quiet, the ideal material for use in the toughest environment. Rubber comes in a wonderful range of bold primaries and neutral tones, as well as different textures like studs and treadplates for extra grip underfoot. Some companies will also offer a color-matching service.

Rubber tiles are easy to cut, so you can create unique patterns and designs. They are laid using an approved adhesive, and expert installation is advised – once cut, the material cannot be repaired if the size is wrong. Alternatively, a "poured" rubber floor will create an even tougher, seam-free surface. This must be carried out by an expert and given adequate time to "set."

To clean, simply mop with water or a gentle detergent, but remember, dirt may get trapped around the relief pattern of textured floors.

Cork A cork floor is warm, comfortable, lightweight, and quiet underfoot. As well as natural hues, cork tiles are now available in a range of colors and with a tough vinyl coating featuring photographic images such as leaves, pebbles, and grass. Tiles are simple to install, using basic do-it-yourself skills. Natural cork needs sealing to prevent wear and staining, but a PVC-coated version requires no special finishing, just cleaning with a damp mop and mild detergent. A hard wax finish creates an extra warm, anti-slip surface.

Carpet While carpet isn't generally recommended for use in the kitchen for practical reasons, coir or sisal matting, made from natural fibers such as coconut husks and agave plants, are far more resilient and hardwearing. Liquid spills can be prevented from soaking in immediately by pre-treating the flooring to create a protective, invisible shield around the fibers. Natural floor coverings will stain, however, so soak up the spillage promptly – dab the stain rather than rubbing it. For normal day-to-day cleaning, use a cylinder vacuum cleaner or the hard floor setting on an upright vacuum. Never use a steam cleaner.

As an alternative to wall-to-wall carpet, hardwearing carpet tiles, made from polypropylene or nylon, are easy to cut and lay yourself. They have a special backing so underlay is not required, but prompt treatment is the most successful course of action for spillages. Carpet tiles, commonly associated with offices and public areas, have currently undergone a revival, with new, ultra-modern designs such as urban pavement, denim, and spots.

Metal Sheet metal or tiles in aluminum or steel will add a distinctive industrial edge to your kitchen, although they can hard on tired feet. Non-slip "tread plate" surfaces are the most practical. The tiles can be glued onto a flat wooden or concrete subfloor; if the floor is not level you should lay Masonite or ¼in plywood to flatten the surface first. Steel is harder than aluminum, although it will rust unless galvanized or powder-coated. Aluminum tiles should not be grouted, as they are difficult to clean afterward. Avoid leaving liquid on the surface for a long duration and re-polish when necessary using liquid polish and a soft cloth.

FAR LEFT: Metal tread plates are hardwearing, industrial and very practical. The change of floor materials from warm wood to cold metal is a bold demarcation of the different areas. **LEFT:** Bright blue rubber flooring is offset by this neon pink kitchen. Rubber tiles are good for kitchens used by children, being warm and extremely practical – and less harsh on the feet and knees than harder floors.

CABINETS

The style of kitchen furniture you choose will have a large impact on the look and feel of the room. If you opt for a built-in kitchen, the cabinets can be designed to fit the room's dimensions. There are three basic units: the lower cabinets, which incorporate sinks, built-in appliances, and storage (either a series of drawers; a cupboard; or a cupboard with one drawer above); tall units with room for shelves, pull-out pantries, or appliances; and upper cabinets, which can have matching door fronts or glass panels for displaying crockery and glassware, for example. Some kitchens, especially smaller rooms, benefit from replacing upper cabinets with open shelving. This will help to open up the space, relieving any feelings of claustrophobia – although it does call for extra tidiness. An unfitted or "modular" kitchen is based around movable, freestanding cabinets, which are designed to resemble pieces of furniture, such as a dresser or tallboy.

Budget kitchens generally offer less choice in terms of style and range of cabinet sizes, which may leave space-wasting gaps in your plan. However, more and more manufacturers are devising flexible approaches, allowing you to mix and match door fronts and create special features such as an angled breakfast bar or stepped island

unit. Remember that stock kitchen cabinets are less expensive and readily available. If you aren't keen on any of the door styles, consider buying off-the-peg carcases and commissioning doors from a carpenter. This way you can get the look you desire, yet still keep costs down.

Mid-range kitchens offer a broader choice of cabinets, usually in 4in increments with varying heights to make best use of space. Custom kitchens offer the ultimate in customization – at a price. A tailormade kitchen isn't limited by any size or precedent, so you will get custom-made cabinets to accommodate you and your kitchen requirements – whether it's a cabinet with a special silverware drawer or a huge, robust chef's pantry. Upper cabinets can be built to the proportions of the room, while difficult or small spaces can be utilized with "specials" such as wine racks, spice drawers, tray slots, or even window seats.

Behind closed doors

The quality of the material behind the door is just as important as what you see on the outside. It's less a question of style and visibility than of stability and rigidity.

Kitchen carcases (the boxes behind the doors) vary in thickness depending on quality and price. A carcase that is made from ¾in- (18mm-) thick melamine-faced medium-density fiberboard is a good standard to aim for, and is more suitable than solid wood, which can warp or move. Carcases should have solid, rigid backs and fully adjustable legs that can take account of uneven floors and protect cabinets from penetrating damp. Look out for colored carcases that match the color of your doors or pale gray versions that merge "invisibly" into the background (as opposed to a gleamingly bright white), which will also suit the trend for steel and aluminum door fronts. Drawer boxes need to have solid sides and be made of either wood or metal, with strong bases and smooth-action roller runners. The best drawers can glide shut with a push from your hip or foot, and close silently. The most expensive are made of wood with

LEFT: Full-length frosted glass cupboards keep china and tableware free from dust, yet in sight, and work well with the glass skylight and door. **ABOVE:** A striking wall of flush-fitting cupboards with rectangular recess utilizes every inch of space and doubles as a blackboard for leaving messages. The steel tubular extractor fan and black pendant light are dramatic but functional. **ABOVE RIGHT:** Lit above and below, this one-piece block of cabinets seems to float inches from the floor. Behind every door lies hidden storage space or an appliance.

dovetailed joints and waxed wooden runners. Full-extension drawers that extend the entire length of the drawer allow complete access to the contents, with everything to hand. A kick plate can be installed to conceal the legs of lower cabinets or they can be left bare to become part of the kitchen design. This space can also be utilized in small kitchens for extra storage (shallow drawers can hold baking trays, frying pans, or tea towels) or a kick-plate heater.

Kitchen cabinets are either framed or frameless. With a framed face, a rectangular frame outlines the carcase, strengthening it and providing a mount for the door to fit into. In-frame doors are better suited to more traditional, custom designs. A frameless door is cheaper to make. It fits flush with the carcase, is easy to hang, and creates a simple, streamlined look. Metal hinges are stronger and more enduring than plastic and also allow for adjustment; clip-on versions allow greater flexibility as doors can be removed quickly and simply.

The doors

The choice of materials and finishes for cabinet doors has become increasingly sophisticated – from a tough rubber coating to milky glass to ridged aluminum. At the same time, the style of the doors available is becoming much simpler and more streamlined to fit in with the increasingly popular straightforward, no-frills, contemporary design. Before you choose your kitchen cabinets, check that the door front is hardwearing and can withstand a variety of knocks and bangs from repeated opening and closing. It must also be easy to clean, especially if you have young children and animals when muddy paw prints and trails of sticky jam can become a daily occurrence.

Solid wood Use wood that has been kiln-dried or acclimatized over a period of months to the humidity of a kitchen, otherwise cabinets will warp or crack when installed. Slight seasonal cracking is to be expected.

FAR LEFT: A single cube of strong color breaks up the band of cabinets. To minimize glare from the reflective surfaces, the light source is concealed at the top and bottom of the upper cabinets. **CENTER LEFT:** Deep blue units, chunky chrome handles, and a checkerboard tiled flooring gives this kitchen a distinct 1930s feel. **ABOVE LEFT:** A wall of mirrors at the far end of this kitchen creates a space-enhancing illusion. The pale lime green units seem to continue endlessly. **BELOW LEFT:** Simple chrome shell grips on wooden door fronts are timeless and good-looking.

Hardwood doors can be made either from solid wood, which means they will be heavy and expensive, or from a combination of solid frames and veneered center panels. The panel provides extra stability and a more contemporary look, as the center will be one piece of veneer rather than a number of flush planks.

Softwood is much cheaper but can lack an interesting grain, so doors are usually stained or painted. Cedar is popular for drawer linings because of its fresh, lingering aroma. Laminated bamboo is great for use as a kitchen door, because it is very strong and resistant to knocks, and is unlikely to warp or swell as wooden doors can do in the humid conditions of a kitchen.

Veneers A veneer is a thin slice of wood, around 0.8mm, which is adhered to the front and back of a substrate of plywood, particleboard, or medium-density fiberboard under high pressure. It can then be finished with two or three coats of two-part lacquer. Since veneer is made by peeling thin layers of wood from a single log, cabinet doors have a sleek uniformity. They are also less expensive and more stable than solid wood but will create the same effect.

Laminates A high-pressure laminate is made from layers of colored or patterned paper which are fused together under high pressure, finished with a tough melamine top layer and bonded to a medium-density fiberboard substrate. Laminates provide a tough, easy-to-clean surface and come in a wide range of colors and patterns, including metallics and wood effects. Make sure the front and back of the door is covered with laminate for strength and to prevent warping. Laminates should be cleaned with water and mild detergent. Persistent marks can be removed using a suitable cream cleaner, but harsh abrasives must not be used. Low-pressure laminate, known as melamine, is cheaper, thinner, and less durable, and is used to cover carcases.

Lacquers Lacquered cupboards are usually at the top end of the price scale. They are available in a wide variety of colors – from pastel blue to scarlet to rich, chocolate brown – in a satin or high-gloss finish. The lacquer comes in two parts and is mixed prior to application and sprayed onto a medium-density fiberboard door. A number of coats are built up to give the door a tough, resilient finish.

Metals No longer the sole preserve of appliances and counters, metals such as stainless steel, zinc, and aluminum bring a touch of industrial chic to kitchen cabinets, and the result is strong and streamlined. Doors are rarely made from solid metal (which would be extremely costly); instead a thin metal skin (around 0.8mm) is wrapped around a medium-density fiberboard core, and given rounded profiles to eliminate sharp edges. Metals can be polished, matte, sandblasted, brushed, or corrugated, and extra decorative effects can be added with perforations or punch marks, or by brushing. Polished stainless steel is clean and highly reflective but smears easily. Matte aluminum can be anodized; this softer, whiter metal looks good offset with thick, greenish glass. Zinc ages to a nice patina, while copper offers a warmer tinge. Some specialist metal companies can transform your existing kitchen by cladding doors and drawers in the metal of your choice. Many budget ranges also offer a stainless steel-effect laminate, which is much cheaper and easier to keep clean.

Glass Until now, glass was mainly used for center panels in a kitchen door, as a means of decoration to break up a run of solid fronts, and as a way to display crockery and glassware. Glass can be clear, sandblasted, frosted, ribbed, or etched, depending on the look you want.

However, glass has recently come into its own and is now used to create complete kitchen doors, which are streamlined and easy to clean. Doors are made from ¼in-thick toughened glass with color baked onto the back for extra durability. Instead of a handle, a neat circular cutout will offer a streamlined look.

Paint Painted cabinetry allows you to choose literally any color from the spectrum – from exuberant, vibrant shades to paler tones to pure white. Paint can also help create an earthy, lived-in ambience that you may not get with the more modern finishes. The classic, Georgian palette of neutrals – gray, olive, and buttermilk – suits both traditional and contemporary kitchens while rich, strong colors like deep green, Prussian blue, and oxblood red can add an injection of personality into an otherwise neutral look. You may decide to paint a single item, say a hutch or serving table in deep charcoal gray or bright azure to set off a predominantly wooden kitchen. It is wise to experiment with different colors and sample pots before you go ahead – particularly with the bolder shades. Look for manufacturers who also offer a range of specialist decorative techniques, including applying colored glazes, distressing, and stippling. If you buy a hand-painted kitchen from a custom-kitchen manufacturer, it should be sealed with a coat of hardwearing lacquer. HPG is a rubber paint that gives a tough, durable finish and is flat and velvet-smooth to the touch.

You can also revamp old cabinets yourself with a fresh lick of paint, but examine the original surface first. Laminate is smooth and non-porous, making it difficult to paint over – ordinary paints will flake and blister. Use a primer and then a satin-finish paint, both from a range especially for use on laminates. All wood – either bare or painted – needs to be sanded and then primed. Sand to a smooth finish with sandpaper (don't use steel wool), remove the debris with a damp rag, and apply a coat of primer. The primer penetrates the wood and grips the grain, providing a key for the next coat of paint. If you don't prime the wood, you'll get a patchy, uneven finish. Medium-density fiberboard must be primed first, otherwise the surface will soak up the paint like blotting paper. Always use one that is formaldehyde-free, and wear a protective mask when working with it. Wooden doors can also be transformed with a colored varnish. Rub down the surface with a fine sandpaper and wipe down with mineral spirits, then apply varnish with a brush in even strokes along the grain of the wood.

ABOVE LEFT: Pale wooden doors are matched by backsplashes made from identical panels turned on their side. The two pendant lamps continue the parallel lines running through the lower cabinets and backsplashes. ABOVE RIGHT: Interlocking blocks of wood and matte gray door fronts create a subtle pattern without the need for intricate design or bold color. BELOW LEFT: A stainless steel tambour shutter can be pulled right down to the counter to hide small appliances from sight, and keep them out of the reach of children. BELOW RIGHT: For a simple and modern interpretation of the 1950s kitchen, simply thread lengths of washable material onto a slim metal pole.

STORAGE

Storage is a fundamental part of a kitchen. There's no point in having a kitchen that looks fantastic if you have to bend, stretch, and root around in the back of deep, dark cupboards to seek out your basic equipment. Not only will this be deeply irritating, it is also not energy-efficient. No matter how big the kitchen, you can never have enough storage.

Inadequate storage is usually less to do with lack of space and far more to do with careless design and bad organization. So it is important from the outset to decide what you need to store, where you need to store it, and how your kitchen will accommodate your needs. Fortunately, kitchen manufacturers have devised a host of clever behind-the-scenes storage solutions to make even the smallest kitchen an efficient, well-organized space. However, one of the advantages of moving into a new kitchen is the opportunity to throw away all those things you never use and don't need and which simply clutter up your life – less is definitely more when it comes to a working kitchen.

FAR LEFT: Modular storage creates an organized feel, and is at its most effective when it insures there is a place for everything from dried food, herbs, and condiments to candles, plates, and glasses. When not in use, two doors can be closed to shut away the kitchen. **LEFT:** Jams, preserves, and bottles are neatly stored beneath the countertop. Handles are dispensed with, giving way to discreet cutouts instead.

Show or conceal

The kitchen is a place that houses an incredible amount of diverse things – from dried foods to dishpans, soap powders to pet food, fresh fruit to garbage bags. Deciding what is to be concealed behind cupboard doors and what is to be displayed on shelves will affect the appearance of the room and its practicality. Kitchen displays work best when they celebrate the beauty of everyday things. A bowl of ripe lemons or a windowsill lined with homegrown herbs can much more appetizing than an artfully arranged collection of china.

Start with a few basic questions. Decide what you want on display: perhaps a row of wall-hung utensils near your cooking area or open shelving to keep herbs and spices? Or do you prefer a sleek, streamlined look with everything stashed out of sight? Visually speaking, this may suit an open-plan kitchen, part of a one-space loft apartment say, where an uncluttered look won't intrude on the rest of the space. However, fully built-in kitchens where absolutely everything is hidden behind cabinet doors can look too sterile and unlived-in. All the same, over-cluttered kitchens can be muddling and tiring to work in.

The kitchen also contains areas where some of the most regularly used supplies and utensils need to be within easy reach. Only objects used every day, or at least once a week, deserve prime storage space – the areas within easy reach – usually somewhere between knee and eye level.

Decide what you need to be most accessible and arrange your kitchen accordingly. It's largely a matter of common sense – the equipment and utensils that relate to each area of activity should be stored or displayed close by. Logically, pots and pans should be stored near the stove or cooktop with their lids off so that air can circulate, and in a position where dust won't collect inside. Try deep pull-out pan drawers with a separate pan-lid rack, or simply hang them upside down from a hook by the handle.

Wicker baskets slotted in below the counter keep vegetables fresh because they allow the air to circulate underneath. Keep herbs and spices and other essential food close to the food preparation area, but remember that spices become unseasonably bland when stored too near heat. Store crockery in a plate rack over the sink or draining board where it can remain after it has dripped dry, or in cupboards near the dishwasher to avoid having to carry it to and fro.

Try not to use up key spaces on things you use once every week or two. Specialist appliances like ice-cream makers and yogurt makers as well as large party platters can be in the less accessible storage areas, perhaps tucked away in the back of low cupboards, or if used really infrequently, perhaps even out of the kitchen altogether. Don't store bulky or heavy items, such as family-size bottles of fruit juice, too high up or too low down.

Small spaces

Finding room for all your pots, pans, and plates, not to mention food, can be a problem in a small kitchen. Make good use of walls with ceiling-height cabinets, interspersed with open shelving to help create a light, airy atmosphere. Exploit every inch of space with interior racks: full-extension,

BELOW LEFT: Vast lengths of chunky steel shelving marry utility with decorative display. This is a sturdy space, ideal for storing bulk supplies of kitchen essentials. **LEFT:** This unique – and cheap – interpretation of the suspended ceiling rail means pots, pans, and utensils are easily accessible. **BELOW CENTER:** Tailormade storage helps to promotes a well-organized, visual feast for the kitchen. Tightly packed open shelving stands in contrast to the dangly loop of the shower-like faucet and casually strung pots and pans. **BELOW RIGHT:** Neat, uniform cubbyholes are good for keeping tableware and accessories close at hand.

slimline cabinets, corner carousels, and even kick-plate drawers, which fit neatly under lower cabinets. A Magic Corner system is particularly useful and is designed to make full and easily accessible use of those dead spaces in a standard corner unit. Some kitchen manufacturers have also developed extra-deep lower cabinets with space at the back of the counter for a range of accessories, including a pull-down chopping board and spice drawers – an ideal solution for narrow, single-line kitchens.

Pantries

Pantries need not be relegated to memories of a bygone childhood – they offer practical and cost-effective storage solutions, allowing you to see your food supplies at a glance.

The natural coolness of a pantry provides a time-honored way of keeping a wide variety of foods fresh. Away from the heat of the kitchen but without the deep chill of the fridge, the pantry allows certain foods like fruit, tomatoes, and jams to mature and improve with age and keeps many others in good condition for considerable periods of time. The traditional location for a pantry is on the side of the house that never sees the sun, and it should have as many external walls as possible, to make full use of the natural chilling and good ventilation.

Pantries should be rodent-proof, cool, and well lit, and should have easy-to-sweep floors and rows of sturdy shelves. Stone walls, a slate floor, and slate, marble, or tiled shelves are perfect. The ambient temperature can be low enough to preserve vegetables and fruit, game, ham, sausages and salamis, jars of preserves, racks of wine, and the odd leftover for overnight storage. The pantry is also an ideal location to store bulk purchases and to put freshly baked pies, cakes, and cookies to cool, out of sight of inquisitive children and pets.

However, many people today live in houses without pantries, and those who have a basement find it is often too warm to use as a food storage room. In terms of space, a pantry is a luxury for most home owners, although the same basic principle can be adapted to fit out a tall cupboard. Pantry cupboards can be ordered from custom kitchen companies, either as freestanding pieces of furniture or built-in with the rest of the kitchen. They are often double-doored, opening out to reveal shelves, wicker baskets, bread bins, and wine racks.

If you do have the space, there is also the option, popular in Scandinavia, of transforming an existing room or part of a room into a walk-in chilled food store. Air conditioning keeps the temperature at a regulated 41°F. The only limitation is that the temperature of the room where the warm side of the unit is placed cannot be lower than 39°F or higher than 79–81°F at any time.

Wine storage

Wine needs to correctly stored if it is going to last. Few people have the space or the budget to create their own wine cellar, but if you do, it is best ventilated. All wine – red, white, and rose – should be stored lying on its side in a cool, dark place. In the kitchen, beware of storing wine too close to the oven, otherwise the variation in temperature will be too great. Simple wire or wooden racks can be adapted to fit most spaces and will carefully cradle your wine.

Wine enthusiasts will relish the prospect of a specially designed wine storage unit to house their wine collection. These units (which can fit under the counter, much like a fridge) feature two temperature zones which can be set to serve wine at the exact temperature you want as well as set at 55°F to duplicate the ideal storage temperature of wine cellars.

FAR LEFT ABOVE: Narrow, pull-out racks utilize otherwise redundant space. The open, galleried sides allow easy access to the herbs, spices, and bottles and keep them in place when the unit is opened and closed. **FAR LEFT BELOW:** A standard drawer is transformed into a terra-cotta bread crock keeping loaves fresh and moist. **LEFT:** Pale gray cubes of storage conceal everything from sight, even the dishwasher. The integral, lipped handles and large angled lamp maintain the utilitarian, almost office-like effect.

case study: KITCHEN STORAGE

Simplicity can be very difficult to achieve. When Jan and Ann Hagelin commissioned architect Nico Rensch to design the interior of their loft, formerly a Victorian school, they specified a pure white, minimal look, with extensive storage to hide all the clutter of everyday life. The solution was to house all the working areas of the space, from kitchen fixtures and appliances to workstations, behind pristine panels, technically a very demanding exercise in specialist joinery.

LEFT: The main working area of the kitchen, where the kitchen range, sink, and water heater are installed, is screened by a pair of bi-folding doors. **RIGHT:** View looking down the loft space from the kitchen counter to the seating area at the far end. The seating area is raised up on a platform which itself contains yet more storage space. The bedroom is on the mezzanine level, and is accessed by stairs hidden behind dummy panels. The space is heated underfloor.

ABOVE: Bi-folding doors under the mezzanine pull back to reveal a workstation. Fitting and constructing storage for such a seamless look is a very exacting task, particularly taking into account essential service runs for plumbing, underfloor heating, and ventilation. The panels are made of medium-density fiberboard, spray-lacquered white; they close on press catches. A key consideration was to make the effect just as elegant when the panels were open, which meant juggling with conflicting geometries. To the right of the workstation, another panel conceals the main entrance to the loft. **RIGHT:** The central island is medium-density fiberboard, with a Formica top. An inset groove or "shadow gap" makes the top appear to hover over the base, lessening the mass of the island. **FAR RIGHT:** Flooring throughout is a gray Spanish limestone, laid in large square slabs. Together with the all-white color scheme, the result is a luminous, serene space that fully satisfies the clients' brief.

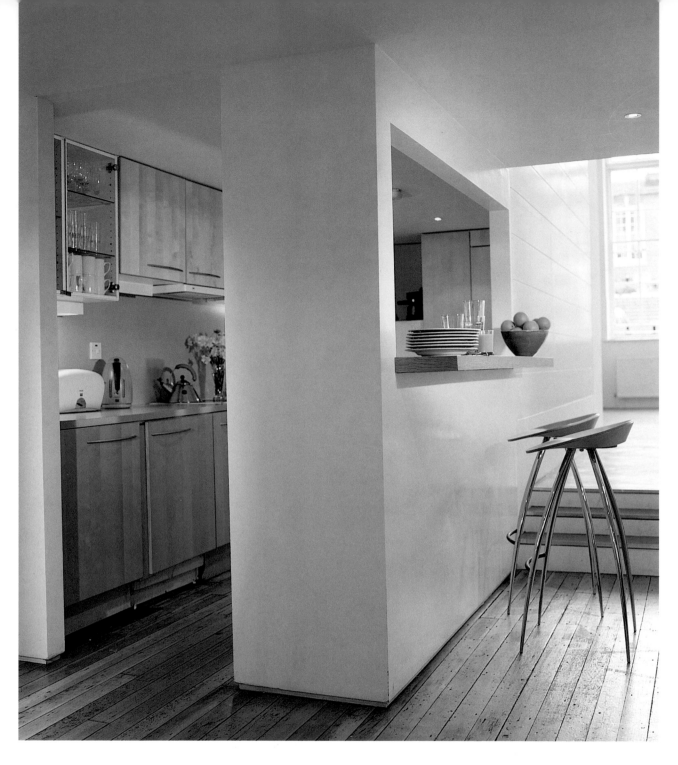

SCREENS AND DIVIDERS

Even though you may like the idea of an inclusive, open-plan kitchen, there will still be times when some form of screening or dividing may be invaluable. It could be a crescendo of whirring appliances or a permanent pile of dirty dishes that instigates such a screening – or perhaps simply a desire to shut oneself off from the rest of the household.

Whatever the reason, decide whether you want a flexible or permanent arrangement. Subdividing part of the kitchen into a utility room will immediately alleviate noise levels. For chefs who prefer to keep their cooking and entertaining separate, hatches allow verbal contact between diners and cooks, but keep meal preparation out of view.

A two-tiered island unit with a raised shelf or backsplash is a practical way of concealing mess on the work side of the kitchen and allows the cook a degree of privacy and concentration. These units provide a subtle separation, instead of brutally segregating the kitchen within an open-plan arrangement – the other half of the island becomes the perfect space for friends and diners to pull up a stool and

LEFT: A narrow galley kitchen is opened up by a simple serving hatch, which also insures the kitchen feels less confined and means that the cook is not excluded from the rest of the room. **BELOW:** In an open-plan space, a two-tiered island unit with a raised shelf successfully hides the cook's handiwork from view. **RIGHT, ABOVE AND BELOW:** This is the ultimate hide-away kitchen. A vast multifunctional living space is cleverly divided up by the use of sliding screens. When the kitchen is screened off, it is still accessible through the ribbed glass door. The colored screen distinguishes the living area from the kitchen space when the screens are closed.

A few steps and a sleek pane of glass subtly demarcate the kitchen from the rest of this space. Clutter can be hidden behind closed doors while minimal fittings and the pale colors enhance the airy, open-plan ambience. **ABOVE RIGHT:** A pivoting wood panel with a tiny, cutout, circular finger pull becomes a modern-day serving hatch. **BELOW RIGHT:** The concrete counter and lilac color scheme from the kitchen have been continued through to the next space to create a modern sideboard in the dining room. The only division is a subtle sandblasted glass panel.

chat to the chef without too much interference. A peninsula unit or breakfast bar is another visual demarcation and can be enhanced by continuing upper cabinets beyond the wall, and mounting them on "legs" so that they sit above the counter. Again, this adds an element of visual privacy yet maintains the fluidity of open-plan living at the same time. Movable shelf or preparation units and bookcases can also hide kitchen mess and allow for more relaxed dining on the other side, while a food preparation unit on casters can be wheeled away when not in use.

To make maximum use of one-space living, site the kitchen along one wall and use sliding or folding panels to screen it off when not in use. Avoid side-hinged doors, unless you have adequate clearance around them for their outward swing. Use transparent materials like sandblasted glass and Plexiglas, which will screen the kitchen from sight, but nevertheless allow daylight to filter through at the same time. Or commission a builder or architect to create a completely "fold-away" kitchen. The doors of the kitchen can be deep, full-height panels, lined on the kitchen side with shelves, and hung using large, very strong hinges to take the weight.

case study: KITCHEN DIVISION

In a converted Victorian industrial workplace, a kitchen
area takes center stage, separated on one side from a dining
area by a bar counter and from the living area on the other by a
freestanding wall. When Dominic Richards bought the east London loft, the
upper level, with its high ceiling supported by exposed roof trusses, had already been
subdivided by a developer into a warren of small boxy rooms, including a galley kitchen.
Dominic, who likes to entertain, opened the space up again to allow the structural bones of the
architecture to show through and enable him to chat to his guests while cooking. A palette of
warm, earthy materials adds a robust sense of character. A wireless system has also been
installed so that a laptop can be used anywhere in the loft.

FAR LEFT: Looking from the dining area straight through to the kitchen. The floor is made of polished oak. Heating is supplied by a low-level coil radiator. **LEFT:** The freestanding wall that encloses the kitchen and separates it from the living area has a long horizontal slit cut into it, positioned just above the work surface to allow views through the space, as well as aiding conversation between areas.

ABOVE: The refectory-style dining table is made of English oak, salvaged from a tree that was brought down in a storm, and set between two broad bands of limestone. A limestone-topped counter, dividing the kitchen from the dining area, provides another eating area.

ABOVE RIGHT: The living area is furnished with generous sofas covered in nubbly wool, and a tufted rug. An integrated sound system allows music to be enjoyed all over the loft. The freestanding wall divides space without blocking views of the spectacular roof structure.

RIGHT: The sleek kitchen is fitted with cabinets faced in medium-density fiberboard. The counters are made of limestone. The panel above the horizontal opening is Indian laurel wood. Concealed downlights in the underside of the cabinets light the work surface.

Appliances have been steadily revolutionizing the kitchen since the 1950s. We now have at our fingertips a host of labor-saving devices that have drastically cut down the time we spend preparing and cooking food as well as liberating us from some of the drudgery of daily chores. They have also become steadily more energy-efficient, and the latest advances in technology even communicate with us and keep us informed at every step. Whether it's to alert us that our cooking time is up or that our fridge door has been left open, these cutting-edge developments have the potential to change the way we live and how we use our kitchens, saving us time and energy like never before.

Fixtures and

Appliances

Equally, fixtures and appliances have become a focus of considerable design interest. Appliances, especially, have ditched their functional, white-box image to become must-have designer-label purchases, as aesthetically pleasing as the cabinets and furniture that make up the rest of the kitchen. From huge stainless steel fridge-freezers to fingerprint-free aluminum washing machines and ranges in rainbow-bright colors like yellow, red, blue, and green, their design is now almost as much of a selling point as their technology and efficiency.

But hi-tech wizardry and high-fashion can be quite a daunting prospect. Before you indulge in needless expense and complexity, ask yourself if an internet-linked fridge or neon pink light-up sink is really going to improve the quality of your life. Technology, when it makes life simpler, when it makes life easier, is an enormous advantage. Decide what range of functions you require, what level of sophistication suits you, and the merits of different sources of power. There are also questions of budget, maintenance, energy savings, and performance to be considered. But remember, a kitchen is for the preparation of food and if you spend more time fiddling with technology and then cleaning that technology afterward, you will actually have defeated the whole purpose of it.

This section sets out what is available in a rapidly changing marketplace so that you can make your own assessment as to whether an appliance is suitable for the kitchen you are planning, the cooking you are planning to do in it, and the money you need to invest to achieve it.

LEFT: Sleek ceramic hotplates set flush with a stainless steel cooktop are as aesthetically pleasing as they are functional. This is a cook center that is not only streamlined and modern in appearance but also very easy to clean. **INSET LEFT:** Everyday kitchen gadgets should be reliable and long-lasting. Many have also become iconic designs. **RIGHT:** Hidden behind a matching fascia panel, a fully integrated dishwasher is a time-saving boon in today's kitchen. Storing plates and dishes nearby allows for easy transfer from the dishwasher.

Choose appliances that not only meet your practical needs, but also fit in with your kitchen style. A simple gas cooktop and an "invisible" extractor fan create a neat, unobtrusive cooking area in this incredibly simple, all-white kitchen.

STOVES, OVENS, AND COOKTOPS

When it comes to the kitchen's primary function – cooking – you want a high-quality, brand-name appliance. This way you can be assured of a sound investment with reliable, long-lasting performance. If you know what brand you want, many leading appliance manufacturers employ home economists who will give free cooking demonstrations at their head showrooms. If you're undecided about a specific brand or model, then visit some of the many kitchen showrooms that have a wide range of working machines and can arrange demonstration days to show the benefits of each appliance.

Stoves

An all-in-one freestanding stove with four electric or gas burners on top, and one or two ovens below, is still the most cost-effective cooking appliance on the market. This type of stove can stand alone or slot in between two cabinets and is easy and cheap to install. (To accommodate a separate built-in oven and cooktop, you may have to rip out your cabinets and start from scratch.) Moreover, you can easily upgrade your freestanding stove, as most come in standard widths, and should slot smoothly into the space of your old model. For very small kitchens, narrow stoves are available, or you could consider a table-top version with two rings and an oven.

There is now a much wider selection of these "entry-level" stoves on the market, with hi-tech features and sleek metal finishes to rival the built-in machines – multifunction fan ovens, wok burners, dual-fuel models (electric oven, gas cooktop), and plenty of safety features. Broilers are usually set inside the oven, which does restrict your ability to roast and grill at the same time; a separate broiler cavity or double oven is a more flexible solution.

Ranges

The popularity of large ranges has been partly fueled by cooking programs on TV, which have linked them to the world of high-profile professional cooks, but also by the huge diversity of ranges that are now available. Whether it's industrial stainless steel or the traditional cast-iron farmhouse range, these sturdy appliances now form the centerpiece of many kitchens, whether traditional or modern.

Enameled, cast-iron ranges like Agas run off natural or bottled LP (liquefied petroleum) gas, oil, electricity, or solid fuel. They release heat through the ovens and hotplates in a consistent way, without the need for a direct heat source. This radiant heat preserves all the flavor, moisture, and texture of food. There are generally two ovens, neither of which has a temperature control; one oven is hot, for roasting, and the other is cool, for slow cooking. Four-oven Agas also have a baking oven and a warming oven. The ovens are always on and so do not need to be preheated; this also makes the kitchen particularly inviting in winter. The two hotplates, one for boiling and one for simmering, are also ready to use at any time. The insulated covers keep heat in when the hotplates are not in use. In addition, some ranges can also provide central heating and hot water. Cast-iron ranges must be installed on a solid, level floor that can take the weight of the appliance, usually around 650lb.

Manufacturers of professional catering equipment have introduced domestic ranges so that we can emulate restaurant chefs at home. These robust and powerful stoves are more controllable than the traditional Agas and often provide up to six burners, with a fish-kettle burner, wok burner, and griddle to accommodate even the most inventive cooking. Two large-capacity ovens, a separate broiler, and a warm storage drawer (for warming plates, allowing bread to rise, or storing cooking pans) complete what is the ultimate cook centre for the serious chef.

Such quality does not come cheap, however. Balance its good looks and high performance against how much you will use a range like this and what you cook. Remember also that you'll need a lot more space. Measuring from about 3ft to 5ft in width, they are often deeper as well as wider than a standard range. Unless they are used as freestanding pieces, these ranges often require made-to-measure cupboards.

If, however, you still hanker after a range but don't have the available space or budget, choose a range-style stove. These vary in width but are smaller, with one or two ovens and four hotplates. Although not as powerful or imposing as the real thing, these mini ranges are available in virtually all the colors and trimmings of their big brothers.

Built-in cooking

Choosing a separate built-in oven and cooktop is usually more expensive, but offers greater flexibility for design and practicality. Ovens can be built in under the countertop or at eye level in a cabinet for easy broiling and less bending and lifting. You can also personalize your cooking equipment by mixing fuel types. A gas cooktop and electric oven are still the most popular combination; however, a row of two-burner domino cooktops (as opposed to a standard four-burner cooktop) allows you to customize your cooktop by installing two gas burners and two ceramic hotplates side by side, in addition to other specialist features like a wok ring or barbecue grill.

Ovens

When choosing an oven, try not to be intimidated by industry jargon and hi-tech features. Do your meals consist of one-pot cooking or a combination of methods? And for how many do you cook and what sort of food? Only you know what you cook and therefore what oven will suit you.

Electric There are three types of electric ovens: conventional, fan oven, or multifunction. The basic electric oven with conventional top and bottom heat produces a graded temperature, which is hottest at the top, so the center is the best place to cook your food.

A fan oven draws air in from the oven via a powerful fan, then heats it up and forces it back into the oven cavity. By continuously circulating hot air around the oven, the desired temperature is achieved much more quickly, saving both time and energy, as little or no preheating is required. Heat penetrates food faster and more uniformly, and there are

LEFT: A French range with double oven and gas cooktop offers plenty of capacity and flexibility. The cream enameled doors and brass trim suit the simple, Shaker-style kitchen cabinetry. **INSET LEFT:** The Aga is a classic, time-honored cooking fixture that gets just better with age. The two ovens and two hotplates are kept constantly heated – ready to use at any time. **ABOVE:** Robust and powerful, a cooking range can dominate the kitchen – this is an appliance for the serious cook. The vast extraction pipe keeps the kitchen odor-free.

FAR LEFT: Separate built-in cooking appliances allow flexibility in terms of location and choice of fuel type. The preferred combination is a gas cooktop and electric oven. **CENTER:** Stainless steel remains a stalwart in the kitchen. A tough, hardwearing material, it adds a professional edge to every look, even this daring bold cherry red. **RIGHT:** Cool and architectural, a series of single gas burners set into a marble worktop is the last word in uncluttered sophistication. This minimal, pared-down aesthetic looks as good unused as it does cluttered with the paraphernalia of cooking.

also no cold spots in the cavity, making this oven perfect for batch baking. Fan ovens are fast and economical, but can sometimes be noisy.

Multifunction ovens combine the two cooking methods to give you a really comprehensive appliance. They can include up to 10 different cooking functions including "hot air grilling"' for a rotisserie effect without the need for turning, and "defrost" which circulates unheated air through the oven to cut defrosting times, ideal for delicate items like cream-based gateaux. Other functions allow you to steam, cook pizzas to perfection (crisp base and moist, melting topping), and bake bread. Some top-of-the-range ovens even include a list of pre-programmed recipes. You enter your chosen program (say, leg of lamb cooked from frozen to medium rare), add the weight, and the oven takes care of the rest. It will switch off automatically and finish cooking the dish using residual heat. You can even store your own recipes in the memory. Again, you need to weigh the cost of such an appliance against how useful these features are.

Gas Many top chefs still prefer gas, because it creates a moist atmosphere, keeps food tender, and helps prevent overcooking. It is also perhaps more controllable. Gas ovens create a zoned heat with the center of the oven heating up to the selected gas mark, the top half hotter, and the bottom cooler. Fanned gas systems are also available, offering even temperatures throughout the oven, which save energy by reducing heating up and cooking times.

Cleaning Pyrolytic self-cleaning ovens heat up to 930°F burning any deposits of grime and grease off the walls to leave a fine ash, which is easily wiped away. This takes around 2–3 hours and can be programmed to run overnight using off-peak electricity. For safety reasons, the oven door

locks automatically when cleaning. Catalytic oven liners are covered with a special coating which absorbs grease like blotting paper, until high temperatures during cooking destroy it. These clean only the areas of the interior where they are fitted and you will have to replace the linings periodically. Otherwise look out for smooth, non-porous enamel surfaces that are easy to wipe clean.

Capacity Don't forget to check the cooking capacity of the oven. A 24in-wide single oven has around 14gal of usable space. This will give you two or three cooking shelves at

ABOVE: A row of narrow domino hobs creates a cooking zone that is tailored to the needs of the cook. Here, a deep fat-fryer, gas burners, and a griddle plate are installed side by side to cater for every culinary whim and experiment. **RIGHT:** The look of a range is achieved by building in an extra-wide single oven and cooktop. With a matching stainless steel trim, backsplash, and hood, these appliances look very well integrated into the row of units.

ABOVE: A black ceramic glass cooktop is offset with a steel trim and matching single oven. Some electric cooktops, such as the induction type, are almost as controllable as their gas counterparts. **BELOW LEFT:** Chunky control knobs, robust cast-iron pan rests and gleaming cookware are the ingredients of a modern-day cook center. **BELOW RIGHT:** A freestanding range with two ovens offers greater cooking flexibility for large families. The simple lines of the stainless steel bar handles are echoed on the cabinet doors.

any given time or space for a 30lb turkey (an average-size, family turkey is around half that). Double ovens are more convenient and flexible, allowing you to cook dishes simultaneously at different temperatures. Many feature a smaller second oven with broiler, which, in a 24in-wide oven, offers around 8gal of space. A full-sized double oven measuring 35in high can be built-in only at eye level. If you are hindered by lack of space, a double oven that will fit neatly under the counter measures 28in high. Wider single ovens (for example, 28in or 35in wide) are more versatile and offer up to 30 percent more cooking space than a 24in-wide oven.

Safety If you have small children, don't forget to ask about low-temperature double- or triple-glazed doors. Even when the interior reaches 400°F, the surface stays at around 120°F. A child-safety control will lock all oven functions, while a safety cutout device switches off the heat after a certain time. Eye-level ovens also remain out of the reach of small, inquisitive children.

Cooktops
Manufacturers have been dreaming up a different type of cooktop for every conceivable cooking method. Domino cooktops are by far the most flexible. These modular, two-plate cooktops can be assembled in any configuration to meet your culinary requirements. Choose from two gas burners, two ceramic hotplates, a barbecue grill, a wok ring, a steamer, and even a deep-fat fryer. These can be built in separately or in combination with each other using connecting surfaces. Some even flip up and down independently, allowing you to choose which domino you want to cook with, then flip the others up to free the extra counter space underneath.

Gas This is still the most popular choice for cooktops because it is instant and highly controllable. Most cooktops include a simmer burner (around 1kW), a high-speed burner (around 2.6kW), and two standard burners (around 1.7kW).

A larger five-burner cooktop is even more versatile and usually includes a powerful double- or triple-ringed wok burner (around 3.5kW or 4kW) or a central fish-kettle burner. One useful safety feature to consider is a flame-failure device – if the flame is accidentally extinguished, by a draft, for example, then the gas supply automatically cuts off.

Electric The most basic electric cooktop is the sealed-plate version, but these are slow to heat up and cool down. Ceramic glass cooktops provide a smooth, streamlined surface, set flush with the counter, which means that you can simply wipe it clean. Halogen rings heat up faster than radiant rings but cannot match gas for speed and control. Induction cooktops are the nearest you'll get to gas in terms of controllability and responsiveness, but they don't come cheap. Unlike with standard ceramic cooktops, heat is transferred directly to the bottom of the pan (and hence the contents) and wastes no energy heating the cooking zone or the cooktop. Only certain pans work with an induction cooktop, namely anything that a magnet would stick to, such as cast iron and enameled steel. If you want to experiment with gas and electric, you could try a dual-fuel cooktop, which features two gas burners and two ceramic or halogen rings.

Tepan units are ideal for cooking stir-fries. The large circular stainless steel hotplate is set into a work surface, and when heated, forms a shallow dip in the middle so no liquid can escape. There is also a mobile version which can be wheeled outside for an exotic alternative to the barbecue.

Extractor fans
There's nothing worse than a kitchen filled with strong cooking odors and greasy steam, especially in open-plan spaces, so investing in proper extraction is crucial. There are two types of extractor fans: ducted (extractor) or recirculating. Extractor fans are the most effective system and take grease, steam, and smells outside the house via ducting. It is best to site your extractor near an outside wall for optimum efficiency – manufacturers recommend a maximum ducting length of 16ft on a straight run, deducting

4ft for every 90-degree bend. If, however, you live in a block of apartments without an accesible external wall, you will need a recirculation model. Stale air is drawn in and purified using grease and charcoal filters, before re-entering the kitchen. Most fans can be adapted for both extraction and recirculation systems. Position the hood carefully above your cooktop: too close and the steam may escape around the sides; too far away and the steam may disperse before it reaches it. For gas cooktops, the minimum distance is around 26in; for electric reduce this to 20–22in.

Power levels Too much power is unnecessary. Before choosing a hood for your kitchen work out the volume of the room to be ventilated, by multiplying length x width x height. A good ventilation system will change the air in a room 10 times per hour, so multiply this figure by 10, to give the minimum extraction rate required. Remember to ask about noise levels, particularly important in an open-plan setting. Aim for around 55–60 decibels as a benchmark.

There are many designs available, from brushed steel and glass canopy hoods to built-in telescopic hoods that fit between two overhead cabinets and slide out when in use. Some come with a handy run-on feature that will continue ventilating the cooking area for 10 minutes after you finish cooking.

Microwaves

These appliances have become almost universal in the home, but their use tends to be limited to reheating pre-cooked food and microwave dinners. Many users are

BELOW LEFT: This glass and stainless steel extraction fan is crucial for eliminating unwanted cooking odors, steam and grease, but also adds a sculptural centerpiece to this kitchen. **BELOW CENTER:** A built-in extractor fan whirrs into action when the matching front panel is pulled out – simple, unobtrusive, but, most important, effective. **BELOW RIGHT:** The glass canopy of this circular extractor fan is continued along the length of the counter to provide useful extra shelf space for storing equipment. Metal U-shaped bars are used for hanging utensils while cooking. **RIGHT:** A custom-made extraction unit not only takes away cooking smells and steam, it is also fitted with recessed spotlights for focused task lighting along the island.

unaware of the versatility and real benefits of microwave cooking, which can help retain vitamins, minerals, and color in our foods that can be lost in boiling, for example.

Microwaves use electromagnetic waves to heat food. When they strike the cooking food, the microwaves cause the water molecules within to vibrate at great speed. In turn, friction between these vibrating molecules generates the heat that cooks the food. The heat therefore originates within the food rather than outside it as in a conventional oven or cooktop. Because the vibrating continues after the microwave is switched off, you need to allow standing time when the cooking process is completed. Some machines with a steam button and specially designed "steamer" accessory, allow you to steam-cook rice, vegetables, and fish in your microwave. The water in the base of the steamer reaches boiling point and is then maintained at a simmer throughout the cooking time.

The combination microwave oven integrates fan cooking or a broiler with all the benefits of a microwave. It will produce food that looks traditionally cooked (browned, roasted, or crisped) but using about half the time and energy of conventional cooking. These combination machines are particularly useful as they can double as a traditional oven, should you need extra oven space. If you want to build in a combination microwave with your single oven, make sure

the appliance is installed at a comfortable height so you can reach over the drop-down door (side-opening doors are for standard microwaves). It may be a good idea to build it in below the single oven or on its own below the counter.

Power, performance, and capacity vary according to manufacturer and model. Full-size models usually have an 8–11gal capacity; compact microwaves are great for small kitchens. The important thing to look for is the diameter of the glass turntable (can you fit in awkward-size dishes?). Otherwise a "stirrer" system (usually found on combination microwave ovens) eliminates the need for a turntable.

Some models also come with automatic cooking and defrosting programs and a memory so you can store the cooking times of your favorite recipes. A talking microwave has also been developed to meet the needs of the elderly and visually impaired.

If you want your microwave built into upper or lower cabinets, buy one with proper ventilation that is specifically designed for such installation. An existing microwave can be adapted with special vents and baffles but this kind of customization is costly. Otherwise, freestanding models can sit happily on a counter or shelving unit. They come in a wide range of colors and finishes to suit – cool metals like stainless steel and brushed aluminum; white, bold colors; and even ultra-modern, semi-transparent designs.

Steam ovens

Steam cooking is a quick and easy way to cook and eat healthily, as it retains minerals, vitamins, and moisture better than any other cooking method. Steam ovens work in various different ways, but instead of boiling or immersing food in water, they surround and cook it with steam (a visible white mist containing small water droplets), preserving the natural goodness.

The latest generation of built-in steam ovens includes sleek, hi-tech reinventions of the bulky tabletop pressure cooker. There are two types of steam ovens – those that cook with pressure and those that cook without. A pressurized system is said to cut cooking times by up to 50 percent using temperatures of up to 250°F (good for cooking solid foods like potatoes). Steam is created in a generator outside the airtight food chamber and forced back in, pressure cooking foods very quickly.

Pressure-less steam cooks food under normal atmospheric pressure. It is not as aggressive as a pressure cooker and the food's consistency and natural appearance survive largely unscathed.

Some steam ovens are plumbed directly into the water supply, and after cooking, any residual water automatically drains out the back of the appliance or can be saved for making stock. Other systems do not require any drainage or fixed water connection, and instead use removable water reservoirs which are filled manually with cold water.

If you don't have space for a steam oven, some multifunction ovens feature a steam facility. The steam can be used on its own or in conjunction with other cooking modes (usually fanned or base heat) to create a moist and humid atmosphere that gently seals and enhances the food's natural moisture. A joint of meat thus remains succulent inside with a crisp, brown skin on the outside.

FAR LEFT: Built-in at a more comfortable eye level, this combination microwave mimics the benefits of a traditional oven, such as broiling and browning, but in a fraction of the time. **LEFT:** Microwave ovens are frequently used for reheating ready-made meals and are generally underrated for their ability to cook foods nutritiously. A built-in model should also include suitable ventilation. **ABOVE LEFT:** A built-in steam oven is a luxurious addition to the kitchen's repertoire of appliances – but it can be costly. **ABOVE RIGHT:** Steam cooking helps retain minerals, vitamins, and moisture in our food, and can make a contribution to healthy eating.

FRIDGES AND FREEZERS

Refrigeration has perhaps had a greater impact on our cooking, eating, and shopping habits than almost any technological development. Choose a fridge and freezer based on the size (and potential size) of your family; your work, shopping, and cooking habits; the size and style of your kitchen; and, of course, on your budget.

Fridges vary from the large, side-by-side fridge-freezers with capacious and versatile storage space and built-in crushed ice and water dispensers to unobtrusive built-in appliances that fit neatly beneath the counter and have door panels to match kitchen cabinets. Remember to look at how the space is organized inside your fridge as well as the gross interior volume. Features like height-adjustable shelving, including split-width shelves to accommodate tall bottles, add flexibility and should ideally be made from easy-to-clean, toughened glass. Doors should also offer good storage with removable shelves, extra-deep balconies (holding up to quart containers), and covered dairy compartments. In the freezer, non-tip drawers with solid drawer fronts will keep temperature loss to a minimum.

FAR LEFT: Reminiscent of a 1950s diner, this fridge, with its curved lines and choice of bold, bright colors, has reached an almost iconic status. **INSET LEFT:** Modern fridge-freezers can be used to make a bold statement in the kitchen.
ABOVE: Creating an assortment of useful storage cupboards on an odd-shaped wall influenced this Mondrian-esque design. A jigsaw of orange and turquoise door fronts (which hide a tall fridge and cupboard space) is interspersed with the glint of stainless steel ovens.

Not all food should be stored in the fridge at exactly the same temperature – dairy produce, meat, and fresh fruit and vegetables all have their own optimum storage conditions. That's why some refrigerators feature multi-zone cooling, controlling the temperature and humidity of specific areas so that different foods are chilled to exactly the right temperature. For instance, humidity-controlled salad drawers help food stay crisper while a chiller compartment means perishable goods such as meat and cheese last twice as long. Indicator lights and temperature guides reassure you that food is being safely stored.

As well as conventional upright models, there are also hi-tech fridge and freezer "drawers" that pull out much like a chest of drawers. These designs are perfect for providing extra refrigeration, especially when built-in under an island unit, or for smaller studio apartments where space may be at a premium.

RIGHT: This gleaming hi-tech fridge-freezer incorporates a cold-water and ice dispenser in one of the doors. **CENTER RIGHT:** An expansive, stainless steel fridge-freezer is a classic addition to this predominantly all-white kitchen. **FAR RIGHT:** Side-by-side fridge-freezers can store an enormous amount of food, with both chilled and frozen food compartments at a convenient height.

Technology

Frost-free freezers circulate a stream of cold air through the freezer cavity, freezing food swiftly and preventing ice from building up on shelves and walls. They also prevent food from sticking together and help maintain texture and flavor. Your freezer should carry at least a three-star rating, so you can store pre-frozen food for up to three months.

Intelligent cooling maintains an even temperature control throughout the fridge and will temporarily direct cool air to warmer areas – if, say, the door is left open. In fridge-freezers, look out for dual compressors with two motors that allow you to control the fridge and freezer separately.

Internet-linked fridges look set to transform the kitchen into the true technological nerve center of the home. These multimedia appliances have TV, radio, and internet access from a built-in, touch-screen LCD. It means that while you cook, you can restock your food supplies on-line, look up new recipe ideas and email friends and relatives without having to leave the kitchen. The fridge can also check itself routinely and, if a problem occurs, send an alarm call direct to the service center. In time, it is also likely to tell you what foods have reached their sell-by date and order more for you at the same time!

What do you need?

The refrigerator is an important piece of kitchen equipment so you should ask yourself these key questions before you make a decision:

▸ How often do you shop for fresh food? Do you need more fridge space than freezer space?

▸ Do you want a fridge with a freezer compartment? If you already have a separate freezer, you may not need one. Or you may want a small freezer compartment if, say, the main freezer is kept in the garage.

▸ Do you want a freestanding appliance or a built-in version? Integrated models can be disguised with panels that match kitchen cabinets whereas freestanding fridges are available in almost every color and finish possible – from bold red to pastel blue to sleek aluminum.

▸ If you choose a built-in model, is eye-level height more convenient than under the counter?

Energy labeling

Refrigeration is becoming increasingly energy-efficient. By law, manufacturers must disclose the energy-efficiency of their appliances. Energy labels have existed since 1995 and show how efficient a fridge or freezer is by using a letter rating from A–G. A is the most efficient and signifies low running costs and maximum care for the environment while G is the least efficient. An A-rated fridge is said to cost half as much to run on a yearly basis than an equivalent C-rated appliance. No new fridge or fridge freezer should contain CFCs (chlorofluorocarbons) and HFCs (hydrofluorocarbons) which have been linked to the "greenhouse effect". However, your old fridge may contain them, so dispose wisely – there may also be controls.

DISHWASHERS

When choosing a dishwasher, don't opt for complicated machines with excess gadgets. Be conscious of energy, water, and detergent consumption. At the end of the day what you want is efficiently cleaned and dried dishes. Having said that, dishwashers are deemed to be more cost-effective than washing by hand and it is estimated that we can spend around 300 hours every year washing dishes at the sink. Top-of-the-range dishwashers use just under 4gal of water compared with about 10gal for washing a similar amount by hand. Not only that, but dishwashers are more hygienic and can wash at higher temperatures (up to 160°F) than your hands can tolerate.

Features

Modern dishwashers are very efficient and use surprisingly little water and energy to wash a full load, mainly as a result of sensors, or "fuzzy logic" systems, that allow the machine to "think for itself." The sensors analyze the degree of soiling in the wash water and calculate the best program and temperature to do the dishes as economically and effectively as possible. There is a vast and bewildering range of programs and special features on offer. Intensive, Normal and Eco programs are probably the most widely used, although Quick Wash is handy for small loads and a 100°F program is good for delicate glasses and china.

Machines with two revolving spray arms, fitted top and bottom, wash best, while efficient filter systems remove food and debris from the wash water. Useful features to look out for include flexible interior features such as height-adjustable top baskets that can take large plates, and fold-down plate racks which create space for casserole dishes and large pans. It's also a good idea to consider a machine with an anti-flood system, which switches off the water supply in the event of a leak.

Stainless steel interiors are more durable and less likely to take on odors or to stain than enamel. However, some metals, such as copper and silver, may discolor because of a reaction to the steel.

ABOVE: Dishwashers ease the aftermath of gatherings. The range of styles and matching door fronts means that they can be made to merge with your kitchen cabinets.

Energy and noise

Energy labels allow you to work out the energy and water costs for a wash cycle. The label shows efficiency and cleaning and drying performance, rated A to G, with A being the best. Triple-A-rated dishwashers are becoming more widely available.

Make sure the operating noise is a barely audible hum. Sound is measured in decibels and the average dishwasher emits around 45–49dB. Look for something around 42dB – which is quieter than a teaboiling kettle – to help maintain a peaceful, relaxing environment.

Size

Dishwashers come in two main sizes: a full-size 24in or slimline 18in. The full-size models take approximately 12 place settings and slimline models around eight (one place setting equals ten pieces of crockery and cutlery). There are also compact, countertop versions, which are said to be able to handle dishwashing for a party of five.

Choose a freestanding dishwasher if you don't want the built-in look. A fully integrated model will be completely concealed behind a full-length cabinet door with the control panels hidden on the inside top rim of the door. Semi-integrated units have the control panels on show.

LAUNDRY

If you have the space, a separate washing machine and dryer will give you the most flexibility, allowing you to dry one full load while washing another.

Washing machines

The average machine uses 60 percent of the water and 40 percent of the electricity that it would have needed 10 years ago. This is down to "fuzzy logic" technology, a computer chip that monitors every procedure and basically "thinks" for you. For each load, it senses the correct wash time, decides which way to wash, and uses the precise amount of water for the best results. It can even detect any excess detergent and add more water should it need to. This way, the amounts of water and electricity required are always at a minimum. Most washing machines take an 11lb load but some models have a 15lb drum capacity, which is handy for larger families and can save time, money, and effort. Bigger porthole doors which open at a 180-degree angle flat against the machine are easier for loading and unloading washing.

Recent innovations include a washing machine that features two drums rotating in opposite directions at once. It was designed to replicate handwashing after research showed that 15 minutes of handwashing got clothes cleaner than 67 minutes in the best washing machine. Another design has introduced a removable wash tub. The idea is that you can color code your dirty clothes with different-colored plastic tubs (i.e. green tub for whites, blue for coloreds); then your chosen laundry basket can be placed straight into the machine. When the wash is finished, the tub is removed and the entire load taken straight to the clothesline or the dryer. It is supposed to ease loading and unloading and prevent the risk of rogue socks staying in the drum and potentially infiltrating the whites wash.

Aim for a machine with an A energy efficiency rating to cut electricity usage and an A wash performance to tackle the worst and most stubborn stains. Triple-A-rated machines also offer excellent spin efficiency, guaranteeing a drier fabric for reduced drying time. If you use a dryer, choosing a washing machine with A-rated spin, instead of one with a G-rated spin, will halve your drying costs. Spin speeds can range from a gentle 400 rpm up to a vigorous 1,600 rpm. As far as programs are concerned, a low-temperature Hand Wash program is useful for any clothes with a "handwash" label, while Short Wash can reduce the length of a main wash program by around 50 minutes. If you wish to take advantage of any lower electricity tariffs at night, delay time features allow you to program the machine to start up to 19 hours later.

You also need to decide between a front loader and a top loader. Top loaders take up less space and some people find them kinder on the back, because you don't have to bend down so far. A standard washing machine is 60cm deep, but shallower models are also available. These are great for a small kitchen, utility room, or older kitchen, where narrower work surfaces can't always accommodate regular-sized appliances.

Dryers

These are available as traditional vented machines or condenser models. Vented dryers are cheap and fast. Hot damp air is vented from the machine to the outside via a hose, so it needs to be sited on an external wall, which can restrict room planning. A condenser system is slower but the appliance can be fitted anywhere. These dryers use a heat exchanger to convert hot air to water which then is collected in a special reservoir. Some models even have an indicator to remind you when the container needs emptying.

Washer-dryers

Combined washer-dryers are good if space is limited, although they can only dry half the washload at a time. Overloading the machine in the drying mode will prevent the contents from drying properly, will cause creases, and may even lead to a breakdown.

Assess noise levels before you buy. Special insulating panels around the machine cabinet and base can be installed to reduce noise. Built-in machines are also quieter.

SMALL APPLIANCES AND BASIC EQUIPMENT

As well as large appliances, kitchens are also home to numerous smaller pieces of equipment and gadgets. Many of these have been the focus of immense design interest, and shops are filled with rows of gleaming saucepans, retro-style toasters, sleek espresso coffee makers, chrome blenders, and funky bottle openers.

It is not uncommon, however, for a lot of tools and gadgets to end up buried and forgotten at the back of cupboards, taking up valuable storage space. As a sensible rule of thumb, for any item in your kitchen you should be able to justify the burning questions "what does it do?" and "how often do I use it?" Frequently used items should be within easy reach of where they are most needed, preferably on the counter, while rarely used machines are best stored in out-of-reach cupboards and drawers. An appliance garage (a counter-mounted cupboard with a pull-down tambour or roller shutter) is great for stowing less attractive small appliances out of sight.

Basic equipment

Basic kitchen utensils perform specific tasks, functions that will take more time and effort with improvised equipment. You don't need a great many of these tools, but the following are indispensable in any kitchen: a lemon squeezer, sieve, funnel, colander, carving fork, can opener, corkscrew, potato peeler, potato masher, apple corer, whisk, ladle, basting spoon, spatula, wooden spoon, rolling pin, pastry spatula, pastry brush (avoid one with nylon bristles), cheese grater, salt bowl, pepper mill, teakettle, and a large, sturdy chopping board (the best are made from end-grain maple). All of these perform very specific tasks that are difficult to improvise and will certainly take you longer and require a great deal more effort if you don't have the right tool at hand. A pair of sharp kitchen scissors will serve as both poultry shears and herb snippers, and can also be used to trim fat or the stems of cut flowers, clip recipes, cut through packaging, and perform other general duties.

A good set of well-made chefs' knives is vital and will make food preparation as effortless as possible. You will need three – in 3in, 5in, and 8in sizes – along with some skewers, a carving knife, and a bread knife with a serrated edge. Carbon steel blades last the longest but will need to be carefully dried and cared for to prevent rusting. Stainless steel blades will not corrode but are harder to sharpen. Store your knives safely in a block, rack, or magnetic holder that can be attached to a wall above the countertop and out of reach of small children. Invest in a butcher's steel so you can quickly and simply keep the blades in best working condition – sharp knives are much safer than dull ones. Ask a professional if you are unsure how to use it.

Your basic equipment should include a range of good-quality saucepans in different sizes so you can cater for different amounts of food and types of cooking. Stainless steel pans are a good choice as they are easy to clean. Look for heavy, ground bases as they diffuse the heat evenly and help prevent food from sticking and burning. The sides of the pans should be quite high so that food can be stirred and liquid ingredients can be easily added at later stages. Make sure that lids are tight-fitting for efficient simmering. Copper pans are more of a rarity these days, but they are attractive to display and good conductors of heat.

A roasting pan is a must in most kitchens; non-stick pans are coated to resist fat and to ease cleaning. You will also need a frying pan and an omelet pan. To protect the non-stick surface, avoid using metal implements, which might scratch and damage the finish. Instead, use wood, plastic, or carbon fiber utensils.

Steel pans can be expensive but beware of aluminum pans, which can affect the flavor and color of certain foods. Cast-iron casserole dishes are perfect for slow cooking and are handsome enough to take to the table. Judge the size you will need according to the number of people you

RIGHT: Every kitchen should have a basic set of kitchen tools and utensils that perform specific tasks, and they should be easily accessible from the cooking area.

LEFT: A magnetic knife holder situated on the wall at the back of the counter is convenient for cooks, while keeping them out of the reach of small children. **BELOW:** Basic utensils such as a whisk and a cheese grater in hardwearing, long-lasting materials are a must for every kitchen – necessary for even the simplest meals. **RIGHT:** Movable hooks attached to a long hanging rail allow those frequently used cooking implements and ingredients to be located within easy reach of the cook.

regularly cook for, but if in doubt, err on the generous side. Casseroles, in particular, will reduce in bulk as they stew, but the raw ingredients can take up a surprising amount of space. When new, cast-iron should be seasoned before use. To season, paint the surface with vegetable oil and place the pan in a moderate oven for half an hour. Remove from the oven, leave to cool, and then repeat the process twice more. To clean the pan, wipe it clean with a paper towel or wash it hot water, but do not use detergent, which will break down the protective coating.

Wok cooking has become increasingly popular and allows you to cook a healthy stir-fry quickly and simply. Some are preseasoned which cuts out the process of deep cleaning and repeated heating and oiling. They may come with a handy round steam rack and domed cover to keep juices in.

Keen cooks will also want adequate baking equipment, – a couple of pudding bowls and cake pans and pie pans in different sizes, a loaf pan, a deep pie dish, a soufflé mold, a quiche pan with a removable bottom, and pastry cutters. Just about everybody needs a large mixing bowl, and a set of measuring cups and a measuring jug will insure you get the quantities exactly right.

Small appliances

There are so many desirable small appliances on the market that you may be tempted to buy more than you need. Ask yourself how often you would use a certain machine and assess whether you have the space to store it. Not only that, but some small machines come with a vast range of accessories which can be time-consuming to wash, so find out also whether the various parts are dishwasher proof.

A good food processor can improve and speed up food preparation, and can be used as a blender for soups and smoothies; some also come with a detachable grinder for coffee beans and nuts. However, you should ask yourself whether the tasks for which you would use a bulky food processor could be done more quickly and with less dishwashing using a selection of individual machines instead

or even a good, sharp knife. Perhaps buying a blender would be more useful and less cumbersome than a multifunction food processor.

A toaster is a staple appliance in the kitchen these days, but make sure you choose one that can toast different thicknesses of bread as well as English muffins, bagels and waffles. Do you have time to prepare freshly squeezed orange juice? If so, would you prefer a manual, hand-lever squeezer or a small, efficient electric juicer? Coffee lovers may want to invest in a state-of-the-art cappuccino and espresso machine (expensive built-in versions are also available); otherwise, a stove-top coffeepot can do the job perfectly adequately.

Other specialist machines such as a pasta maker, bread maker, ice-cream maker, and yogurt maker will depend on your cooking habits and expertise as well as the available storage space in your kitchen.

SINKS AND FAUCETS

Sinks

Even if you have a dishwasher to deal with your stack of dirty dishes, you still need a good kitchen sink to rinse, fill, drain, wash dishes by hand, and prepare food. Choose a sink based on function, space, and style. Whether you want one, two, or three bowls depends on your work habits, available space, and budget. A large single sink, roomy enough for oversize pans and chopping boards, may be enough if you do have a dishwasher, but make sure your largest pan can fit into it easily – take the pan into showrooms if necessary. However, a double or one-and-a-half bowl (one small bowl between the main sink and drainer) is good for washing and rinsing at the same time. Triple sinks will need lots of counter space and may incorporate a garbage disposer in the center. Round sinks look visually attractive but do not make best use of available space (although they can be a good secondary sink for vegetable preparation) while an L-shaped sink maximizes space by fitting into a corner unit. Flexible, multifunction sinks are becoming more popular. These large- capacity sinks can accommodate an enormous amount of crockery, pots, and pans, good for large families who do not have a dishwasher or for post-dinner-party chaos. For everyday use and smaller amounts of dirty dishes, the sink's dimensions can be halved using a removable wall divider or bowl insert.

The style of your sink and the material it is made from should fit in with the look of your kitchen. Inset sinks are probably the most common type, where the lip of the sink stands ⅛in or so above the counter and is sealed with a waterproof edge. More convenient and hygienic are flush-mounted versions which are seamlessly installed with the counter. There are no edges or seams to harbor dirt or bacteria, and liquids can be wiped straight from the counter into the sink. Undermounted, rimless sinks are set under stone or wood, while integral sinks are made of the same material as the counter, most commonly stainless steel or solid surfacing such as Corian, to give a neat, one-piece finish.

To tie in with the trend for modular kitchens, freestanding sink units are fast becoming popular. Like something straight out of a commercial kitchen, these workstations on legs feature a chunky slab of stainless steel with a bowl and drainer on top, and a shelf below.

Materials

Stainless steel remains a popular choice for sinks. It is tough, resists rust, corrosion, and heat, and can withstand sudden temperature changes. It is also extremely hygienic. Better sinks contain more nickel, giving the sinks a richer luster, warmer color, better cleanability, and resistance to water spotting and scratches. A high-quality 18/10 grade has 18 percent chromium and 10 percent nickel added during manufacture to make the stainless steel rust-proof. The thicker the gauge, the quieter and sturdier the sink. An 18 gauge steel is the best choice for domestic use while the thicker, 16 gauge is for commercial applications. Thinner, 20 and 22 gauges will be noisier and tinnier and could possibly flex when heavy pans are put in them. A highly polished finish is more likely to show up scratches than brushed, satin, and textured versions. Other metal sinks include white bronze (an alloy of copper, manganese, and zinc), brass, sandcast aluminum, and copper. Each gives a warmer nuance than steel.

Ceramic sinks have a natural high-glaze finish that is functional and good-looking. Large, oblong apron sinks of porcelain-coated fireclay suit both traditional and modern country kitchens. These sinks can be set on top of kitchen cabinets or wall-mounted using supporting brackets. Modern-style ceramic sinks with an inset design suit the more contemporary kitchen. Cast-iron sinks with thick layers of porcelain enamel fused on top retain their lustrous finish and sparkle for years with proper care. The smooth

RIGHT: The most successful kitchens mix and match fixtures and fittings to create a unique look. Here a deep, oblong apron sink is inset into the modern chocolate brown cabinets for a vibrant new version of the country kitchen.

ABOVE: Limestone is most widely recognized in colors such as soft cream, buff, and sand, but here a pebble-gray limestone countertop is the perfect foil to the apron sink and modern chrome tap. RIGHT: A block of dark greenish gray Corian has been formed into a deep, rectangular sink with a seamless, one-piece backsplash and work surface. The chunky pale wood legs emphasize the simplicity and solidity of the washstation.

CENTER RIGHT: The kitchen sink has been transformed into a multifunction preparation center with sliding chopping boards and a lidded cutout positioned above a trash can for disposing of food scraps and peelings.

FAR RIGHT: A seamless, one-piece sink and countertop in stainless steel means there are no dirt traps for bacteria.

non-porous surface is resistant to chips, stains, scratches, soap, and food acids while the inherent strength of cast-iron enables the sinks to be made larger and deeper without danger of flexing. They come in as many colors as paint.

Synthetic sinks are made of composite materials containing a mix of resin, acrylic, and natural stone particles such as granite and quartz. They are warm to the touch and durable and can resist extremely high temperatures, dents, chips, and stains. Basically, the higher the stone content, the tougher the sink. These are available in a wide selection of plain colors and granite effects.

Corian and other solid surface materials are sleek, modern, and expensive. The sinks come as an integral bowl molded seamlessly into a counter of the same material, with the option of a carved-out drainer.

A wooden sink will lend understated luxury and warmth to any style of kitchen. These are made from teak in simple square designs and are incredibly warm and tactile. The wood reduces the noise of clattering dishes and naturally inhibits bacterial growth, while a laminated teak base prevents leakage.

New innovations include a light-up translucent sink made from tough polymer in a range of zesty colors including lime, lemon, and bright pink. It features a touch-sensitive disc that turns the light on or off and antibacterial protection.

Sinks are not just for washing dishes. With the help of some extra accessories such as slide-over chopping boards, wire baskets, drainers, and colanders, the humble kitchen sink is quickly transformed into a multifunction workstation, which is brilliant for the smaller kitchen.

Faucets

These are among the most hardworking, frequently used elements of your kitchen. With them you fill sinks, buckets, and saucepans, rinse dishes before they go in the dishwasher, wash your hands, and rinse vegetables. Kitchen faucets are constantly in use, so it is crucial that you select the correct model. Which type is best for you rests with your personal preference and the style of your kitchen. There is a huge choice available, including sophisticated, hands-free versions which turn on and off when heat sensors detect your hands underneath. A faucet with a swing spout integrates hot and cold water into the single spout, allowing you to get exactly the right temperature. Single-lever versions control the flow and temperature of the water with one easy-to-use lever. Pillar faucets keep temperatures separate with two fixtures, one for hot and one for cold, while bridge types have separate hot and cold faucets joined to a central spout by a bar. Both styles look good with traditional sinks such as apron sinks.

A pull-out spray spout with an extendable hose is useful for rinsing pots, pans, and dishes before they go into the dishwasher and for washing surfaces around the sink. For someone who suffers from arthritis, lever faucets are a good option as they can be turned on with an elbow or forearm. A tall, swan-neck spout facilitates filling tall pots and buckets. To release space on the sink or counter, wall-mounted faucets are a good idea, especially if they have an adjustable spout.

Look for a faucet that can be turned fully on or off with just a quarter-turn (90 degree) movement, rather than a full 360 degrees. Also, drip-free ceramic-disc technology is far better than a faucet that relies on a washer to control the flow of water. Faucets cast of solid brass (copper and zinc) will give maximum corrosion resistance, whereas mid-price faucets are often made from recycled brass, and those at the lower end of the price scale are usually plastic.

Faucets come in many finishes, including chrome (brushed, matte, and high-polish), brass, epoxy coatings (tough, smooth, and in many colors), pewter, and nickel.

Water filters

If you drink a great deal of bottled water, you may want to install an integral water filter as an alternative. This self-contained unit is tucked away under the sink and purifies the cold water as it passes through the system, taking out any sediment, rust, scale, and chemicals. Such a three-way faucet dispenses hot and cold water (independently or mixed) and has an extra lever on the faucet body to operate the purification system. The special ceramic cartridges provide around six months' worth of purified water.

BELOW LEFT: A custom-made triangular sink utilizes unused space beneath the kitchen window. It is finished off with a single-lever faucet, which controls both the temperature and the flow of the water.
BELOW RIGHT: Two circular stainless steel bowls are undermounted beneath a green stone counter, while a bridge faucet with two traditionally styled handles adds elegance.
RIGHT: The tactile, earthiness of this thick, pale-toned concrete counter is offset with a simple stainless steel sink and a chrome, swan-necked faucet.

GARBAGE DISPOSAL

Waste is an unavoidable by-product of human existence. The problem is that there is so much of it. Even the smallest household produces a staggering amount of garbage. Regulations on garbage disposal vary from country to country. In Germany, residents are required by law to separate rubbish. Here in the United States, recycling mandates vary from city to city, state to state.

It is estimated that around 25 percent of household garbage is food. For those with a garden or field, compost heaps can be a great way to recycle vegetable leftovers. However, protein waste such as meat, fish, and dairy products should not be composted, as they can produce harmful airborne pathogens while rotting down.

Garbage disposers

Most homes in the United States have an electric garbage disposer and 80 percent of all new homes have one fitted. They fit underneath the sink waste outlet and get rid of food scraps including bones, nuts, eggshells, and fruit. Garbage is fed into the disposer with water from the cold faucet and converted into a fine slush that goes into the drains. Depending on where you live, it is then recycled with other organic waste as agricultural fertilizer.

There are no knives or blades in this system. A spinning metal plate pushes the food against a tough grind-ring attached to the wall of the food chamber. The waste is ground safely to fine particles and flushed out through the drainage pipes. Quiet motors have been developed to keep noise to a minimum while compact units leave plenty of storage space under the sink.

There are two types of garbage disposers. A continuous-feed model is always open, allowing a steady stream of food garbage to be fed into the disposer as it operates. It is controlled by a switch on the wall or work surface. A batch feed will operate only when a special sink plug is inserted into the disposer after the garbage has been fed in. Turning the plug starts and stops the disposer; the waste is therefore processed a batch at a time. This is safer for small children and prevents teaspoons from going down the spout, but it is more expensive.

Trash compactors

Trash compactors are already common in American households, but if you don't have one yet and you have a large family, you may want to consider one.

LEFT: Dedicated storage space is the key to making recycling as simple and effortless as possible. Plastic, stackable bins beneath the counter are as effective as sophisticated garbage disposal systems.

RIGHT: Separating recyclable trash into different categories is environmentally responsible. Semi-transparent plastic storage bins with lids allow you to see what is being stored in each container.

FAR LEFT: An adjoining utility room or porch can be ideal for storing both your trash and recycling containers. The trash collected can then be easily transported outside for collection or taken to a central recycling depot. **LEFT:** This pull-out waste storage unit has been subdivided into smaller bins for collecting different types of materials.

These trash compactor machines can reduce rubbish to a far more manageable size – less than one-quarter of its original bulk – and compress it into tidy square bundles wrapped in paper sacks. Compactors can either be portable or attached under the counter and can be used to compress non-biodegradables and packaging materials such as cardboard and plastic containers. They can also be used for recycling purposes if you restrict them to crushing only one type of trash – aluminum cans or newspapers, for example. However they can be expensive, and the compressed bundles can take a long time to decompose. It may be better to flatten cans by stamping on them or using a mechanical press. Either way, aluminum cans take an estimated 80–100 years to degrade and plastic bags 10–20 years. To help minimize the trash that goes into your bin, always try to select products with the least amount of packaging, and reuse containers, bags, and other items wherever possible.

Recycling

Separating trash into different categories ready for recycling is environmentally responsible. Many households are already required by law to separate waste into paper, biodegradables, glass, and metals – and those who are not are encouraged to do so in order to protect the environment.

The key to separating trash is creating the space to do so. You should also find the most convenient recycling point. The waste may be collected from your home on a designated day, or you might have to take it to a depot.

Waste sorting systems that fit below the worktop make it extremely easy to organize household waste. These pull-out drawer systems are divided into separate, removable bins for collecting different types of materials. Otherwise, make room for stacks of newspapers, magazines, and printed matter, and boxes of bottles and glass, in a garage, shed, or spare cupboard. Stash them in containers that can be easily transported to the collection point.

Resources

The preceding sections provided inspiration, information and ideas to help you equip and design your kitchen to your specification. In these pages, we provide more in-depth details of some of the more practical elements, such as what questions to ask your dealer when buying a kitchen, crucial safety information, and advice on measuring up. There is also a budget planner for you to plan your finances accurately and advice on work schedules. Finally, there is a comprehensive list of suppliers as a basis for your research.

BUDGET PLANNER

The cost of remodeling a kitchen will depend on many variables: individual needs, style of life, priorities, and budget. The size of the room is another factor, but do bear in mind that the smallest kitchen can cost twice as much as a huge one – it all depends on the quality and cost of fixtures. Ask yourself how important the kitchen is to you and your family – is it a well-used room, the real hub of family life, or is it somewhere just to reheat the occasional meal? How you use your kitchen will translate into how much you wish to spend on it. The amount you spend must also relate to the value of the property in which the kitchen will live.

However large or small your budget, the most important thing is to stick to it. The best way to keep track of what you've spent and to avoid potential hidden costs is to break down every single element of your project.

What it can cost:

► Initial consultation and kitchen plan
► Structural work
► Rewiring and relocating utilities
► Lighting
► Heating
► Flooring
► Kitchen units:
    Cabinets
    Shelving
    Fittings
► Handles/knobs/pulls
► Counters
► Backsplash
► Sink and faucets
► Appliances:
    Oven, cooktop, and extractor fan
    Fridge and freezer
    Microwave
    Dishwasher
    Laundry appliances
    Garbage disposer
► Decoration – materials and labor
► Delivery of kitchen
► Installation of kitchen

By budgeting for these elements, you should be able to avoid hidden costs and stay within budget. If you do go over budget, you can easily rethink certain elements if necessary. For example, you could substitute a very expensive stone floor with a poured and painted concrete one or tackle the decoration yourself rather than hiring a professional. However, never skimp on important costs such as an electrician's and a plumber's fees and the installation of your kitchen.

Before you start, prioritize your needs according to what you will value in a kitchen: don't splash out on a terrazzo countertop if you can't afford to buy a refrigerator. Everyone will have different priorities. A keen cook may sacrifice the luxury of a dryer and chic designer door knobs in favor of a robust, powerful range, whereas large-capacity laundry appliances may be top of the list for big families. Make a list of your priorities and an inventory of what you have in your existing kitchen. You may be able to reuse certain elements or sell on others to raise extra cash for your new purchase. And be realistic: if you haven't got a huge budget, glass surfaces and a built-in steam oven may be out of the question.

Terence

Conran

Consultant editors: Elizabeth Wilhide, Lara Sargent

Publishing director: Lorraine Dickey
Senior editor: Muna Reyal
Creative director: Leslie Harrington, Lucy Gowans
Designer: Carl Hodson
Picture researcher: Clare Limpus
Special photography: Winfried Heinze
Styling for special photography: Sally Hayden, Sylvie Jones
Production director: Zoe Fawcett, Adam Smith
Senior production controller: Manjit Sihra

Text copyright © 2002 by Conran Octopus
Book design and layout copyright © 2002 by Conran Octopus
Special photography copyright © 2002 by Conran Octopus

Published by Clarkson Potter/Publishers, New York, New York.
Member of the Crown Publishing Group, a division of Random
House, Inc.
www.randomhouse.com

Originally published in Great Britain by Conran Octopus Limited
in 2002.

CLARKSON N. POTTER is a trademark and POTTER and
colophon are registered trademarks of Random House, Inc.

Printed in China

Library of Congress Cataloging-in-Publication Data is available
upon request.

ISBN 0-609-61052-X

10 9 8 7 6 5 4 3 2 1

First American Edition

ACKNOWLEDGEMENTS

The publisher would like to thank the following photographers, agencies and architects for their kind permission to reproduce the photographs in this book:

1 Hotze Eisma/Taverne Agency;2 Verne Fotografie; 3-4 Tom Nagy/La Casa de Marie Claire/Picture Press (Stoeppler + Stoeppler Architekten BDA); 6 left Patrik Engquist (Architect: John Pawson); 6 right Winfried Heinze/Conran Octopus; 7 left Lisa Linder/House & Garden/The Condé Nast publications Ltd (Designer:Olga Polizzi); 7 centre & right Winfried Heinze/Conran Octopus; 8-9 Anthony Browell; 10 David Woolley/Elle Decoration (Architect: Ken Shuttleworth); 12 left Marie Pierre Morel/Stylist:Christian Puech/Marie Claire Maison; 12 right Hotze Eisma/Taverne Agency; 13 left Eduardo Munzo/The Interior Archive (Architect: David Mikhail); 13 right Chris Gascoigne/View (Fletcher Priest Architects); 14 Designer: Norbert Wangen; 15 left Henry Wilson/The Interior Archive (Architect:Voon Yee Wong; 15 right Rien Bazen/'Tile Kitchen' design: Arnout Visser, Peter van der Jagt & Erik Jan Kwakkel, 'Handy Burner' design: Peter vander Jagt, both for for Droog Design, 2001; 16 Patrik Engquist (Architect: John Pawson); 18 left Clive Frost; 18-19 Nigel Noyes; 19 right Ken Hayden/Red Cover (Designer: Jonathan Reed); 20 Minh & Wass; 22 Jennifer Cawley; 23 Victoria Gomez/Living etc/IPC Syndication; 24-25 Stefano Azario/Elle Decoration; 25 right Pia Tryde/Homes & Garden/IPC Syndication; 26 Bulthaup; 27 Verity Welstead/Red Cover; 28 above Tim James/View (Architect: Julian Arendt Associates; 28 below Jake Fitzjones/Red Cover (Fulham Kitchens); 30 Jean-Francois Jaussaud; 31 Jennifer Cawley; 32 Patrik Engquist; 33 Guy Obijn; 34 Jennifer Cawley; 35 Verne Fotografie; 36-39 Robin Chanda (Stephen Turvil Architects); 41 Stellan Herner; 42 left Richard Powers; 42 right Giulio Oriani/Vega MG; 44-45 James Mitchell/Red Cover; 45 right Tom Scott (Azman Owen Architects); 46 left Ray Main/Mainstream; 46 right Gianni Basso/Vega MG; 47 above Dennis Gilbert/View (Blanel Architects); 47 below Daniel Hertzell; 48-49 Peter Cook/View (Architect: Magyar Marsoni); 49 left Andreas von Einsiedel/Red Cover; 49 right Richard Powers; 50 above Tim Clinch/The Interior Archive (Designer: Henry Brougham); 50 below left Graham Atkins-Huges/Red Cover; 50 below right Jan Baldwin; 51 James Morris/Axiom Photographic Agency; 52-53 Antoine Bootz/Stylist: D. Rozensztroch/Marie Claire Maison (Architect: Deborah Berke); 53 Paul Ryan/International Interiors (Architect: Deborah Berke); 55 Winfried.Heinze/Conran Octopus; 56 Guy Obijn; 57 left Tim Young/Living etc/IPC Syndication; 57 right Jean-Francois Jaussaud; 61 Winfried Heinze/Conran Octopus; 62 Deidi von Schaewen (Designer:Jeff Sayre); 63 Kim Sayer/Red Cover; 64 Grazia Branco/Iketrade; 65 Patrik Engquist (Architect: Claessons, Koivisto & Rune); 66 Ray Main/Mainstream (Designer:Andrew Martin); 67 left Ray Main/Mainstream (Designer:Andrew Martin); 67 right Jan Baldwin; 68 above left Eduardo Munzo/The Interior Archive; 68 below left Verity Welstead/ Red Cover; 68-69 Luke White/Elle Decoration; 70 Deidi von Schaewen; 71 left Graham Atkins-Hughs/Red Cover; 71 right Per Gunnarsson/Stylist: Annette Ekjord; 72 above Richard Glover/View (Interior Designer: Deborah Francis); 72 below Per Gunnarsson/Stylist: Annelie Törngren; 73 Minh & Wass; 74- 75 Winfried Heinze/Red Cover; 76 Jan Baldwin; 77 Gianni basso/Vega MG; 78 Peter Cook/View (Tugman Architects); 79 Verne Fotografie; 80-81 Eduardo Munzo/The Interior Archive (Architect: Seth Stein); 80 below Giulio Oriani/Vega MG; 81 below Verity Welstead/Red Cover; 82 Winfried Heinze/Red Cover; 83 Patrik Engquist; 84 Eric Morin/World of Interiors; 85 above Christoph Kicherer (Architect:Briffa Phillips); 85 below Grazia Branco/Iketrade; 86 left Architect: Nico Rensch; 86 right Giulio Oriani/Vega MG; 87 Per Gunnarsson/Stylist:Annelie Törngren; 88 left Giorgio Possenti/Vega MG; 88 right Giulio Oriani/Vega MG; 89 Sven Everaert (Architects: Claire Bataille & Paul Ibens); 91 (Architect: Misha Stefan); 92 Simon Upton/World of Interiors; 93 Mirjam Bleeker /Stylist: Frank Visser/Taverne Agency; 94 Tom Mannion/World of Interiors; 94 below Marie-Pierre Morel/Stylist: Marie Kali/Marie Claire Maison; 96 above left Eric Morin; 96 above right Jean-Francois Jaussaud; 96 below Giorgio Possenti/Vega MG; 97 Jan Baldwin; 99 James Mitchell/Red Cover; 100 above Guy Obijn; 100 below Fulham Kitchens; 101 Ken Hayden/Red Cover; 103 left Jake Fitzjones; 103 right Jean-Marc Palisse/Madame Figaro (Designer:Aude Cardinale); 103 below right Eduardo Munzo/The Interior Archive; 104-105 Patrik Engquist (architect: Claessons, Koivisto + Rune); 106 above Stefan Muller-Naumann; 106 below Ken Hayden/Red Cover (Architect: John Pawson); 107 left David Sandison (Designer: Gail Hinkley); 107 right David Sandison (Architect: Gabriel Poole); 108 Eric Morin; 109 above Thomas Stewart/ IPC Syndication (Architect: Mooarc); 109 below left Maire-Pierre Morel/ Stylist:Puech & Postic/Marie Claire Maison; 109 below right Giorgio Possenti/Vega MG; 110-115 Winfried Heinze/Conran Octopus; 117 Lisa Linder/House & Garden/Condé Nast Publications Ltd (Designer: Olga Polizzi); 118 above Jennifer Cawley; 118 below Santi Caleca; 119 Verne Fotografie; 120-121 Grazia Branco/Iketrade; 121 above Patrik Engquist/ Architect: Erik Andersson & Magnus Ståhl); 121 below Deidi von Schaewen; 122 below left IMS Bildbyra; 122 below right Giorgio Possenti/Vega MG; 123 above Ricard Powers/Elle Decoration/stylist:Kate Ebben (Architect: Lara Gosling); 124 Giulio Oriani/Vega MG; 125 above Paul Ryan/International Interiors; 125 below Jan Verlinde; 126-127 Mirjam Bleeker/ Stylist: Frank Visser/Taverne Agency; 127 above Stellan Herner/ Stylist: Synnöve Mork; 127 below Ed Reeve/ The Interior Archive; 128 left Grazia Branco/Iketrade; 128 above right Andreas von Einsiedel/Red Cover; 128 below right Giorgio Possenti/Vega MG; 130-131 Michael Moran (Moneo Brock Architects); 133 James Morris/Axiom Photographic Agency (Architect: John Pawson); 134 left Jake Fitzjones/Red Cover; 134 right Guy Obijn; 135 left Per Gunnarsson/Stylist:Annelie Törngren; 135 right Jan Baldwin (Architect: Jonathan Clark); 137 above left Stellan Herner; 137 above right Verity Welstead/ Red Cover; 137 below Trevor Richards/ Abode; 138 Wayne Vincent/The Interior Archive; 139 left Giulio Oriani/Vega MG; 139 right Giorgio Possenti/Vega MG; 140 above Giorgio Possenti/Vega MG; 140 below left Alexander van Berge; 140 below centre Giulio Oriani/Vega MG; 140 below right Per Gunnarsson/ Stylist: Annette Ekjord; 142 left Peter Cook/View (Architect: Ludwig Mies Van Der Rohe); 142 right Eric Morin; 143 James Morris/Axiom Photographic Agency; 144 left Paul Grootes/ VTWonen/Sanoma Syndication; 144 right Chris Everard; 146 below Keith Collie (Architect: Azman Owen Architects); 146-147 Deidi von Schaewen; 147 right Richard Powers (Stephen Turvil Architects); 148 Peter Cook/View (Architect: Jonathan Woolf); 149 left Daniel Hertzell; 149 above right Guy Obijn; 149 below right Jake Fitzjones; 151 above left Deidi von Schaewen; 151 above right Nick Carter (ARK Architects); 151 below left Patrik Engquist/IMS Bildbyra; 151 below right Giulio Oriani/Vega MG; 152-153 Guy Obijn; 153 left Trevor Richards/Abode; 154 Marianna Wahlsten/Elle Decoration/ Stylist: Michelle Ogundehin; 155 above James Morris/Axiom Photographic Agency (Architect: Paxton Locker); 155 below left Jean-Francois Jaussaud; 155 below right Grazia Branco/Iketrade; 156 above left Neil Davis/Elizabeth Whiting & Associates; 156 below left Bulthaup; 156 right Taverne Agency; 158-161 Eduardo Munoz/The Interior Archive (Architect: Nico Rensch); 162 Graham Atkin-Hughes/Red Cover; 163 above Pere Peris/La Casa Marie Claire/Picture Press; 163 below left Winfried Heinze/ Red Cover; 163 below right Pere Peris/Picture Press/La Casa Marie Claire; 164-165 Guy Obijn; 165 above right Hotze Eisma/Stylist:Riane Landstra/Taverne Agency; 165 below right Richard Powers/Elle Decoration (Architect: Lara Gosling);166-169 Ray Main/Mainstream (Designer: Dominic Richards); 171 Winfried Heinze/Conran Octopus; 172 above Patrik Engquist; 172 below Winfried Heinze/Conran Octopus; 173 Daniel Hertzell; 174 Hotze Eisma/Taverne Agency; 176-177 Daniel Hertzell; 177 above Jan Baldwin; 177 below Steve Dalton/Red Cover; 178 left Ray Main/Mainstream (Designer: Andrew Martin); 178-179 Luke White/ The Interior Archive; 179 right James Morris/Axiom Photographic Agency (Architect:Claudio Silvestrin); 180 Alexander van Berge; 181 Hotze Eisma/ Taverne Agency; 182 above Chris Evans/Red Cover; 182 below left Per Gunnarsson/Stylist:Annelie Törngren; 182 below right Nick Carter; 184 left Ake E:son Lindman (Wingådhs Architects); ; 184 centre Simon Whitmore/Living etc/IPC Syndication; 184 right Mona Gundersen; 185 Paul Grootes/VT Wonen/Sanoma Syndication; 186 left Ray Main/ Mainstream; 186 right Richard Powers; 187 left Alexander van Berge; 187 right Dennis Brandsma/VT Wonen/Sanoma Syndication; 188 Eigen Huis & Interiors/Sanoma Syndication; 189 above Jake Fitzjones; 189 below Ray Main/Mainstream; 190 Alexander van Berge; 191 left Giulio Oriani/Vega MG; 191 right Robin Chanda (Stephen Turvil Architects); 192-194 Winfried Heinze/ Conran 196 left Solvi Dos Santos; 196 right Winfried Heinze/Conran Octopus; 197 Daniel Hertzell; 199 Winfried Heinze/Red Cover; 200 above Linda Hancock/Plain English; 200 below Ken Hayden/Red Cover; 201 left Guy Obijn; 201 right Rene Gonkel/Eigen Huis & Interiors/Sanoma Syndication; 202 left James Morris/Axiom Photographic Agency (Littman Goddard Hogarth Architects) ;202 right Deidi von Schaewen; 203 Hotze Eisma/Taverne Agency; 204 Daniel Hertzell; 205 Per Magnus Persson/Johnér Bildbyrå/ Photonica; 206 Daniel Hertzell; 207 Bulthaup; 209-224 Winfried Heinze/ Conran Octopus.

Pages 112 /114 Painting by Mark Upton.

223

ACKNOWLEDGEMENTS

BUYER'S QUESTIONNAIRE

Remodeling a kitchen can be the most expensive purchase you ever make – after your home and car. It's a big financial commitment, so you need to insure that the money and time you invest will get you the kitchen you want, both in terms of design and function. Of course budgetary constraints will pay a large part, but whether you're buying a ready-to-assemble kitchen from a home center or commissioning a carpenter to make a one-off design tailored specifically to your needs, there are some crucial questions you should ask your potential kitchen retailer before you sign on the dotted line. Be aware that staff at home centers may not be as knowledgeable as the kitchen specialists, so you may need to do more research yourself.

Questions to ask

Is the company a member of a recognized trade body? A trade association will give you peace of mind that the business has been checked and approved and can offer protection against bankruptcy or any disputes. Look for logos in a store window or simply ask.

What does the price include? Ask for a detailed written quotation that covers every aspect of the job including installing, tiling, flooring, and any structural alterations you have discussed. Don't be afraid to question the price if the original quote isn't within your budget. For example, a cheaper countertop material and less expensive appliances may dramatically affect the total.

How much deposit will I have to pay? Nearly all showrooms ask for some sort of deposit – but never pay the full amount when you place your order. A deposit of around 25 percent is normal; anything higher than 40 percent is suspicious. And do not sign anything unless you are prepared to honor your side of the sales contract. Some retailers have expensive cancellation clauses.

Is there a free design service? Most showrooms offer this as a free service but check to see that an extra charge isn't added onto your total bill. It is more likely that custom-kitchen designers will charge you for plans.

How long will the job take? Find out when the cabinets are due to arrive and how long they will take to install. Get a written estimate of this for extra peace of mind.

How strong are the cabinets? Look at showroom cabinets and inspect how sturdy the furniture is. Don't be afraid to pull open drawers and doors and inspect areas that receive the heaviest wear, such as edges and hinges. Find out what the carcases are made of.

Can I see previous installations or speak to previous customers? This is crucial if you are buying a tailormade kitchen. Only then can you get an overall feel for the company and fully inspect the workmanship and quality of the cabinetry. At the very least, ask to see a portfolio of work.

Do you offer a full aftersales service? Ask if the company offers any written guarantees – against faulty fixtures and appliances and shoddy workmanship. If they also installed the cabinets for you, do they inspect when installation is complete?

Questions a retailer should ask you

It's not only you who should be armed with a list of questions when remodeling a kitchen. Any reputable retailer should also have many questions to find out about your home and lifestyle. Judge a kitchen company by how many of the following you are asked.

When can I make a site visit? Independent retailers and custom-kitchen companies should always visit your home before they give a firm quotation. This way, they can accurately measure the kitchen, plan the layout, and work out what building work may be required. Be wary of those who do not visit your home. Having said that, it is unlikely that larger outlets like home centers will offer a site survey, so you need to be prepared with accurate measurements yourself.

What do you like and dislike about your present kitchen? Finding out what works well and what doesn't can help a retailer design a kitchen to suit your exact specifications.

What is your budget? It's no good planning a blow-the-budget kitchen if you haven't got a huge amount of cash to spend. Fixing a budget before the design process begins is crucial. And don't assume that a specialist kitchen shop is an expensive option; a good retailer should be able to work within your budget and still give you the kitchen you want. But bear in mind that custom kitchens are a lot pricier.

Lifestyle questions

▶ Who will use the kitchen? Do you have children or pets?
▶ Is anyone in the family elderly or disabled?
▶ Do you want somewhere to eat in the kitchen – a table or breakfast bar? Do you want to hold dinner parties there?
▶ Apart from cooking and preparation, what else is your kitchen used for? Laundry, ironing, homework, entertaining?
▶ What style would you like your kitchen to be? What colors, flooring, and wall coverings do you prefer?
▶ How much storage do you need? Do you want open shelving or closed cupboard space, built-in or freestanding?
▶ What kind of appliances do you want? Freestanding or built-in? And what type of fuel do you plan to use?
▶ Are you planning an addition to your kitchen? Are there any structural items in place?

SAFETY HINTS AND TIPS

Don't forget the safety aspect of your kitchen. This is a room full of sharp utensils and hot appliances, a lethal combination that can lead to accidents if you aren't vigilant. However, by incorporating a few simple safety precautions into your design, you can avoid potential disasters.

Cooking appliances

▶ Try to buy appliances with built-in safety features such as a child-lock button on a cooktop to prevent children from turning on the heat by accident.

▶ A gas cooktop with a flame-failure device will automatically cut out the gas supply if a pan boils over or a sudden gust of wind accidentally blows out the flame.

▶ Look out for double- or triple-glazed oven doors, which keep them cool to touch.

▶ Non-tilt oven shelves (also called telescopic

shelves) won't tip over even if you have a heavy casserole dish resting at the end.

▶ Shorten cords on small appliances or replace with the curly type to prevent children accidentally pulling on any which might overhang the counter. Never trail cords across a sink or cooktop. Install electrical switches and outlets well away from the water source.

▶ Flank all the cooking areas with a heat-resistant countertop material such as stainless steel or granite.

▶ Install stoves and cooktops away from windows – drafts may blow out gas flames and curtains may catch fire if the burners are near a window.

Cooling and washing

▶ Fridges and freezers fitted with door alarms to alert you if the door isn't closed properly are useful. Leaving a door open will allow internal temperatures to rise and food to spoil, potentially leading to food poisoning.

▶ Fridges should be set between 32°F and 41°F and freezers at 0°F.

▶ Fridges and freezers should be located away from extreme temperatures so they can work efficiently. Don't locate a fridge-freezer in a garage unless you have a separate thermostat for the freezer, and don't site a fridge next to a heat source such as a radiator or oven – it will have to over-compensate and use more energy.

▶ Understand the star ratings on your freezer and frozen food. One star means frozen food can be stored for one week; two stars means frozen food can be stored for one month; three stars means frozen food can be stored for three months; and four stars means fresh food can be frozen.

▶ Door locks on washing machines are essential to prevent children from pulling doors open and crawling inside the machines.

Planning

▶ Consider ergonomics. Don't put the cooktop and sink at opposite ends of the kitchen with the oven off at a tangent – running across the room with hot, heavy dishes and cooking oils could cause not only havoc, but also potential disasters.

▶ Look after your back by storing heavy items such as casserole dishes and small appliances in lower cabinets or shelves and lighter ones like glassware and packages in upper cabinets.

▶ Deep drawers with non-slip bases or an upright peg system will allow crockery to be stored without sliding around as the drawer is opened and closed.

▶ If the fridge is on the other side of the room to the oven or chopping surface, invest in a mobile chopping block so you can take out all the food you need in one trip. This will help to avoid not just too many return trips across the room, but also lowering the temperature of the fridge by constantly opening and closing the door.

Other

▶ Avoid sharp corners on counters, replacing them with a rounded or axis profile.

▶ Good task lighting is crucial – all work surfaces and cooking areas must be well lit.

▶ Fit child locks on any cupboards containing chemicals, cleaning substances, knives, or other potentially dangerous objects.

▶ All kitchens should have a fire extinguisher and fire blanket in case of fire.

▶ Choose a non-slip material for floors, and wipe up spills immediately.

▶ If paint was applied to a surface in your kitchen before 1980, there is a 50 percent chance it contains lead. Investigate and replace if necessary.

▶ If you do any deep fat frying, learn how to put out a fat fire.

MEASURING

Once you have outlined all your requirements to your dealer or designer, the next stage is planning and allocating the space available. Most retailers and custom-kitchen companies will accurately measure your kitchen during an initial site visit. However, if you buy your kitchen from a home center you may need to provide the measurements of the room and the positions of fixtures and essential services yourself (see illustration above). Accuracy is vital as built-ins have only small margins of error. You will need graph paper, a pencil, ruler, and tape measure. Choose a convenient scale, using metric or standard measurements, depending on the unit size. Consider the following points as you draw up your scale plan:

▶ Measure the width and height of each wall and the distance from the end of the wall to doors and windows.

▶ Draw in the position and size of any permanent fixtures such as doors and windows, showing which way they open and also sill heights.

▶ Measure any projections such as radiators, air vents, and pipes – their width, height, and distance from wall.

▶ Show the position of gas and water supply points, electrical outlets, and fuse boxes.

You may wish to tackle the layout of the kitchen as well. Cut out pieces of paper to scale to represent the sink, stove, and fridge, and arrange them into a work triangle that you think will work for you (see above). Don't position your oven or cooktop too close to a room door, where someone at the stove might be hit by the door; neither should you fit cabinets above the cooking area unless you fit an extractor fan. To prevent a feeling of claustrophobia, the overhead cabinets shouldn't be too low, especially around eating areas, and, if you are positioning your fridge or freezer next to the oven, make sure there is adequate insulation between them.

Place the rest of the kitchen on the graph paper. It helps to use tracing paper over the graph paper and draw the emerging floor plan in bold lines so you can see it take shape. Alternatively, you could experiment on your computer using one of the many software programs that are now available for kitchen design.

Another way to visualize your kitchen layout is to draw each wall to scale (called an elevation, see above). This shows a front view of the cabinets, oven, sink, and so on. It will help you to avoid any jarring changes in height and to spot potential problems such as placing the fridge or washing machine in a corner where access will be awkward. Usually the final design is a synthesis of plans and elevations.

You could also label your plans with the colors, materials, and appliances you have chosen. So you can keep a track of the cost, choose a variety of products and materials and label them "good," "better," "best," and "the ultimate." This way you can easily scale back to control costs by substituting an expensive item for something less pricey: for example, replacing granite countertops with a laminate look-alike.

WORK SCHEDULE

Once you've chosen and ordered your new kitchen, it is essential that you put together a work schedule, particularly if the room is having a complete overhaul. Do you know when the tiles are arriving, for instance, and should the flooring go down before the cabinets are installed? However large or small, a new kitchen means disruption and inconvenience to your daily routine so preparation is key.

Before you start

A good-quality kitchen installation may take around one to two weeks, but if you've chosen a tailormade design with extensive redecoration and reconfiguring of space, expect disruption to last up to 14 weeks. You may need to set up a temporary kitchen in another part of the house. If so, make sure the room has access to water, and keep portable appliances such as a toaster and microwave on hand.

The kitchen must be completely cleared of everything prior to installation. Pack up everything that won't be used in your temporary kitchen, then label the boxes and put them out of the way. As well as food, remove drawers, spice racks, clocks, curtains, and accessories, and allocate good storage beforehand to minimize clutter. Place a protective sheet over existing floor coverings and anything that must remain in place while the work goes on. If you've chosen a rigid kitchen (as opposed to a ready-to-assemble version that will arrive in boxes) make sure you have adequate floor space for it to stand on – ideally, not impeding the installation area itself. Also, do not forget to make arrangements for the disposal of trash that will accumulate during the work. If you need to rent a dumpster, do so in plenty of time and check whether you need to obtain a permit if the skip is standing directly on the road outside your house, instead of on a private driveway. And finally you may wish to advise neighbors of any major building work that is about to take place.

Removing appliances

Before removing any major appliances, turn off all utilities. If the law requires, schedule a specified professionally qualified body to install gas appliances. If you are unsure about electricity, call in a qualified electrician. Use carpet samples or pieces of cardboard to slide appliances out of position – it will also help to protect the floor from gouges or scratches. Most refrigerators need only to be unplugged – a fridge or freezer can simply be plugged into a socket in another room, without even emptying. If it has an icemaker, you will need to locate the water supply valve (usually under the sink) and shut it off before disconnecting the supply tube. Don't stock the fridge or freezer if your electricity supply is going to be cut off.

Plumbing matters

Depending on what level of installation you choose, your team of installers may also strip out your old cabinets. If not, disconnect the sink before you tackle removing the cabinets. Shut off the water supply at the valves below the sink and turn the faucets on to drain the water lines. Remove the clips underneath the sink that secure it to the countertop. An old cast iron sink will be much heavier than stainless steel or porcelain and will need an extra pair of hands when removing it.

Removing old cabinets

The next stage is the removal of counters and cabinets. Remove the emptied drawers and take off the doors from all the cabinets, then unscrew the counter from underneath the lower cabinets. If it has been glued down, you may need to use a crowbar to lever the counter off, but remember to protect the wall by sliding a piece of wood between the wall and the crowbar. Tackle the lower cabinets first so it will be easier to get underneath the upper cabinets. The lower ones are usually attached to each other through the sides of the cabinet front and to the back wall using screws (although older types may be nailed in place). Remove all screws and lift the cabinet away from the wall. The upper cabinets are attached to each other and the wall in a similar way – remove the screws and the cabinets will come out.

Making good

Once the kitchen is cleared, this is a good time to undertake any preparatory work. If you need to relocate/add electrical outlets, water, or waste or gas pipes, or if extensive structural work is included in your plans, it should take place now. Make sure you schedule contractors in advance. Otherwise, while there are no cabinets or appliances in the kitchen, it is the ideal time to patch and repair walls. You can even apply a primer and first coat of paint.

Floors

If you are planning to replace the floor covering, it is best to do so before the new cabinets are installed. This way, it will run from wall to wall, underneath the cabinets. Hardwood and ceramic tiles are always laid before cabinets are installed as they will raise the height of the floor, but vinyl flooring can be laid after the cabinets are in place. It is important to patch and repair an existing floor if the new floor is being laid directly on top, to insure a smooth surface.

Sample work schedule

1 Clear the kitchen and store everything you don't need in labeled boxes. If necessary set up a temporary kitchen in a nearby room. Make arrangements for the disposal of trash.

2 Turn off the utilities and remove appliances – call in the professionals if you are unsure.

3 Demolition phase. Disconnect plumbing and remove cabinets. If you are planning to donate or sell your old cabinets, have a place ready for them to go as you take them out.

4 Once the kitchen is clear, major structural work should take priority. Ask for a written schedule of work from all the tradesmen.

5 If there is damp, treat it now.

6 Wiring, plumbing, and gas installation must be completed next.

7 Electric wiring for lights and wall outlets should be done before any plastering.

8 Repair walls and apply primer and the first coat of paint.

9 If you are upgrading the floor covering, do so before the new cabinets are installed. Vinyl flooring can be laid after the cabinetry is in place.

10 Your room is now ready for the installation team to fit the new cabinets.

Suppliers List

Kitchen Designers and Architects

PIERCE ALLEN ARCHITECTS
80 8th Avenue #1604
New York, NY 10011–5126
Tel: (212) 627–5440

BEECH ASSOCIATES
145 East 94th Street
New York, NY 10128–1701
Tel: (212) 876–6554

Furniture and hardware

LEXINGTON FURNITURE INDUSTRIES
3301 Highway 8 South
Lexington, NC 27292
Tel: (336) 357–7939
www.lexfurniture.com

MCGUIRE FURNITURE COMPANY
151 Vermont Street, San Francisco
CA 94103–5039
Tel: (415) 986–0812
www.mcguirefurniture.com

MERIT METAL PRODUCTS
CORPORATION
242 Valley Road
Warrington, PA 18976–2520
Tel: (215) 343–2500
www.meritmetal.com

MODERN OBJECTS
300 Long Beach Boulevard #10
Stratford, CT 06615–7153
Tel: (203) 378–5785

Cabinet Manufacturers

ARISTOKRAFT
1009 North Geiger Street
Huntingburg, IN 47524–8914
Tel: (812) 683–5959
www.aristokraft.com

BULTHAUP USA
153 South Robertson Boulevard
Los Angeles, CA 90048–3207
Tel: (310) 288–3875
www.bulthaupusa.com

KRAFTMAID CABINETRY INC.
16502 Industrial Parkway
Middlesfield, OH 44062–8208
Tel: (440) 632–5333
www.kraftmaid.com

MERILLAT CABINETRY
from: Town and Country
4315 North Adrian Highway 52
Adrian, MI 49221
Tel: Merillat (517) 263–8282
Tel: Town and Country (517) 263–9585
www.merillat.com

PLAIN 'N' FANCY KITCHENS INC.
Oak Street and Route 501 North
Schaefferstown, PA 17088
Tel: (717) 949–6571
www.plainfancycabinetry.com

SCHROCK
217 South Oak Street
Arthur, IL 61911–1242
Tel: (217) 543–3311
www.schrock.com

SIEMATIC CORPORATION
150 East 58th Street Fl 8
New York, NY 10155–0002
Tel: (212) 593–4915
www.siematic.com

SMALLBONE
from: SieMatic Corporation
150 East 58th Street Fl 8
New York, NY 10155–0002
Tel: (212) 593–4915

SNAIDERO INTERNATIONAL USA INC.
8687 Melrose Avenue #G176
West Hollywood, CA 90069–5736
Tel: (310) 657–5497
www.snaiderousa.com

WELLBORN CABINET INC.
38669 Highway 77
Ashland, AL 36251
Tel: (256) 354–7151
www.wellborncabinet.com

WM OHS
WILLIAM OHS SHOWROOMS
115 Madison Street
Denver, CO 80206
Tel: (303) 321-3232
www.wmohs.com

WOODWORKS INC.
7710 West Shawnee Mission Parkway
Shawnee Mission, KS 66202–3061
Tel: (913) 362–2432
thewoodworksinc.com

Countertops

CUSTOM TILE & MARBLE INC.
11001 SW 60th Avenue
Miami, FL 33156
Tel: (305) 667-TILE (8453)
www.customtilemarble.com

ECO TIMBER INTERNATIONAL INC
1020 Heinz Avenue
Berkeley, CA 94710–2719
Tel: (510) 549–3000

FORMICA CORPORATION
1 Mckinley Street
Linden, NJ 07036
Tel: (908) 587–1980
www.formica.com

FORO MARBLE CO.
140 3rd Street
Brooklyn, NY 11231–4823
Tel: (718) 852–2322

FRENCH COUNTRY LIVING
10205 Colvin Run Road
Great Falls, VA 22006–1833
Tel: (703) 759–2245
www.frenchcountry.com

MONARCH TILE SHOWROOM
4321 Bryson Boulevard
Florence, AL 35630–7318
Tel: (256) 718–4121

RYERSON STEEL & ALUMINUM
1465 65th Street
Emeryville, CA 94608–1073
Tel: (510) 653–2933

SYNDESIS (SYNDECRETE)
2908 Colorado Avenue
Santa Monica, CA 90404–3650
Tel: (310) 829–9932
www.syndesisinc.com

VERMONT SOAPSTONE COMPANY
248 Stoughton Pond Road
Perkinsville, VT 05151–9695
Tel: (802) 263–5404
www.vermontsoapstone.com

VERMONT STRUCTURAL SLATE
3 Prospect Street
Fair Haven, VT 05743–1219
Tel: (802) 265–4933
www.vermontstructuralslate.com

WALKER ZANGER
8901 Bradley Avenue
Sun Valley, CA 91352–2602
Tel: (818) 504–0235
www.walkerzanger.com

Flooring

BRUCE HARDWOOD FLOORS
16803 Dallas Parkway
Addison, TX 75001–5215
Tel: (214) 887–2100
www.brucehardwoodfloors.com

COUNTRY FLOORS
613 Marcy Avenue
Brooklyn, NY 11206–6459
Tel: (718) 384–9374
www.countryfloors.com.au

ECO TIMBER INTERNATIONAL INC
1020 Heinz Avenue
Berkeley, CA 94710–2719
Tel: (510) 549–3000

FLORIDA TILE SERVICE CENTER
2210 A-Z Parkway
Lakeland, FL 33810–6878
Tel: (863) 665–4646
www.floridatile.com

HISPANIC DESIGNE
6125 North Cicero Avenue
Chicago, IL 60646–4303
Tel: (773) 725–3100
www.hispanicdesigne.com

KENTUCKY WOOD FLOORS INC.
4200 Reservior Avenue
Louisville, KY 40213–2045
Tel: (502) 451–6024
www.kentuckywood.com

NAFCO INC.
30750 US Highway 72
Hollywood, AL 35752–6114
Tel: (205) 259–3434
www.domco.com

RYERSON STEEL & ALUMINUM
4165 65th Street
Emeryville, CA 94608–1073
Tel: (510) 653–2933

SHEOGA HARDWOOD FLOORING
& PANELING INC.
15320 Burton Windsor Road
Burton, OH 44062–9785
Tel: (440) 834–1710
www.sheogaflooring.com

SUMMITVILLE TILE INC.
State Route 644
Summitville, OH 43962
Tel: (330) 223–1511
www.summitville.com

WALKER ZANGER
8901 Bradley Avenue
Sun Valley, CA 91352–2602
Tel: (818) 504–0235
www.walkerzanger.com

Sinks and Faucets

AMERICAN STANDARD
1 Centennial Avenue #101
Piscataway, NJ 08855–3996
Tel: (732) 980–6000
www.us.amstd.com

CHICAGO FAUCETS
2100 Clearwater Drive
Des Plaines, IL 60018–1918
Tel: (847) 803–5000
www.chicagofaucets.com

DELTA FAUCET COMPANY
55 East 111th Street
Indianapolis, IN 46280–1071
Tel: (317) 848–1812
www.deltafaucet.com

ELKAY MANUFACTURING COMPANY
2222 Camden Court
Oak Brook, IL 60523–1248
Tel: (630) 574–8486
www.elkay.com

GROHE AMERICA INC.
241 Covington Drive
Bloomingdale, IL 60108–3123
Tel: (630) 582–7711
www.groheamerica.com

KOHLER COMPANY
444 Highland Drive
Kohler, WI 53044–1500
Tel: (920) 457–4441
www.kohlerco.com

VANCE INDUSTRIES INC.
250 Wille Road
Des Plaines, IL 60615–5018
Tel: (847) 375–8900

VERMONT SOAPSTONE COMPANY
248 Stoughton Pond Road
Perkinsville, VT 05151–9695
Tel: (802) 263–5404

Appliances

ASKO, INC.
1161 West Executive Drive
Richardson, TX 75081–2230
Tel: (972) 644–8595
www.askousa.com

BROAN
Broan-NuTone LLC
P.O. Box 140
Hartford, WI 53027
Tel: (800) 558-1711
www.broan.com

LA CORNUE FRENCH RANGES
from: Purcell-Murray Co.
113 Park Lane
Brisbane, CA 94005–1311
Tel: (415) 468–6620
www.lacornue.com

DACOR
950 South Raymond Avenue
Pasadena, CA 91109–3275
Tel: (626) 799–1000
www.dacorappl.com

FIVE STAR DIVISION
Brown Stove Works, Inc.
1422 Carolina Avenue NE
Cleveland, TN 37311–2159
Tel: (423) 476–6544
www.fivestarrange.com

FRIGIDAIRE CO.
600 Perimeter Drive
Dublin, OH 43017
Tel: (614) 792–4211
www.frigidaire.com

GARLAND COMMERCIAL INDUSTRIES
185 South Street
Freeland, PA 18224–1916
Tel: (570) 636–1000
www.garland-group.com

JENN-AIR RETAIL & BUILDER SALE
5607 East Washington Street
Indianapolis, IN 46219–6427
Tel: (317) 357–1186
www.jennair.com

MAYTAG APPLIANCES
403 West 4th Street North
Newton, IA 50208
Tel: (641) 792–7000
www.maytag.com

MODERN MAID
Heffner & Washington Street
Topton, PA 19562–4211
Tel: (610) 682–4211

PANASONIC COMPANY
1 Panasonic Way
Secaucus, NJ 07094
Tel: (201) 348–7000
www.panasonic.com

SHARP ELECTRONICS CORP.
Sharp Plaza #1
Mahwah, NJ 07430–1163
Tel: (201) 529–8200
www.sharp-usa.com

SUB-ZERO FREEZER CO., INC.
4717 Hammersley Road
Madison, WI 53711–2798
Tel: (608) 271–2233
www.subzero.com

THERMADOR
5551 Mcfadden Avenue
Huntington Beach, CA 92649–1317
Tel: (714) 901–6600
www.thermador.com

VIKING RANGE CORP.
111West Front Street
Greenwood, MS 38930–4442
Tel: (662) 455–1200
www.vikingrange.com

WOLFRANGE CO.
19600 South Alameda Street
Compton, CA 90221–6291
Tel: (310) 637–3737
www.wolfrange.com

Universal Design

RESOURCE CENTER FOR ACCESSIBLE
LIVING
Architectural Modification Consultation
602 Albany Avenue
Kingston, NY 12401
Tel: (845) 331–0541
www.ddconnections.org/resource.htm

Useful Addresses

ACADEMY OF NATURAL SCIENCES
1900 Benjamin Franklin Parkway
Philadelphia, PA 19103
Tel: (215) 299–1000
www.acnatsci.org

ASSOCIATION OF HOME APPLIANCE
Manufacturers
Suite 402
111 19th Street
NW Washington, DC 20036
Tel: (202) 872–5955
www.aham.org

THE JAMES BEARD FOUNDATION
167 West 12th Street
New York, NY 10011–8297
Tel: (212) 675–4984
www.jamesbeard.org

GAS APPLIANCE MANUFACTURERS'
ASSOCIATION
2107 Wilson Boulevard no.600
Arlington, VA 22201–3042
Tel: (703) 525–7060
www.gamanet.org

HARDWOOD MANUFACTURERS'
ASSOCIATION
400 Penn Center Boulevard
Ste. 530
Pittsburgh, PA 15235-5605
Tel: (412) 829–0770
www.hardwood.org

NATIONAL ASSOCIATION OF PLUMBING,
HEATING AND COOLING CONTRACTORS
180 South Washington Street no.100
Falls Church, VA 22046–2900
Tel: (703) 237–8100

RAINFOREST ALLIANCE
65 Bleeker Street F16
New York, NY 10012–2420
Tel: (212) 677–1900
www.rainforest-alliance.org

THE SMART KITCHEN by David Goldbeck
Published by Ceres press
2585 State Route 212
Woodstock, NY 12498–2115
Tel: (845) 679–5573

WATER QUALITY ASSOCIATION
4151 Naperville Road
Lisle, IL 60532–1088
Tel: (630) 505–0160
www.wqa.org